RECLAIM YOUR WORKDAY

RECLAIM YOUR WORKDAY

Sustainable Productivity Strategies for the New World of Work

By

MARCEY RADER

ISBN: 979-8-89316-466-4 - Paperback
ISBN: 979-8-89316-465-7 - eBook

BONUS RESOURCES!

Want to supercharge your book experience and unlock even more value? Readers who snag our complimentary bonus guide implement and reach their goals faster!

Sign up at reclaimyourworkday.com

Get instant access to our Reclaim Your Workday Go-To Guide with:

- Links to podcast training episodes under 20 minutes to listen to alone or to use as discussion prompts for your team
- The link to a sample Communications Matrix
- Links to bonus videos with actionable tips
- Information on how RaderCo can support you, your team, or your company

Download now and start reclaiming your workday!

Don't miss out! Get your free copy at reclaimyourworkday.com

DEDICATION

To Jen Shevlin, Vice President of Human Resources, and Marie Noel, Senior Director of Total Rewards at Blueprint Medicines—partnering with you since 2019 has been a dream come true. You've set the bar for future collaborations with others because working with you both has been such an incredible experience. You are shining examples, role models, and mentors to so many, often without even knowing it. You've made me a better business owner, but more importantly, a better person.

And to Lisa Wood, RaderCo Client Concierge, Marketing Specialist, and BFF. Hiring you in November 2021 felt almost too good to be true, but not only did it work—it made every day more fun. You've filled the missing piece in the sometimes lonely world of business ownership. From pastries on slides to mastering video editing, you've gone from zero to 60 in a blink. You're the bacon to my eggs and a true diamond.

CONTENTS

INTRODUCTION

In today's fast-paced business environment, productivity and well-being are not just buzzwords but critical components of a successful company. Yet, many organizations continue to struggle with burnout, inefficiency, and disengaged employees. The statistics are staggering:

- 51% of U.S. employees report watching for or actively seeking a new job, putting self-reported turnover risk at its highest level since 2015[1]

- 77% of professionals have experienced burnout at their current job[2]

- 91% of professionals say having an unmanageable amount of stress or frustration can impact the quality of their work[3]

---

[1] Corey Tatel, PhD, and Ben Wigert, PhD, "42% of Employee Turnover is Preventable But Often Ignored," Gallup, July 10, 2024 (https://www.gallup.com/workplace/646538/employee-turnover-preventable-often-ignored.aspx)

[2] "Workplace Burnout Survey," Deloitte, 2018 (https://www2.deloitte.com/us/en/pages/about-deloitte/articles/burnout-survey.html)

[3] "Workplace Burnout Survey," Deloitte, 2018 (https://www2.deloitte.com/us/en/pages/about-deloitte/articles/burnout-survey.html)

xii | MARCEY RADER

- 64% of professionals say they frequently feel stressed or frustrated at their current job[4]

I've experienced this firsthand. Early in my career, I was driven by the relentless pursuit of more—more certifications, more promotions, more athletic pursuits. I paid more attention to shutting down with inbox zero than to the quality of my sleep. It wasn't until I faced two preventable medical diagnoses that I realized the toll this was taking on my health and happiness. This wake-up call led me to reevaluate my approach to work and life and eventually to start a company (RaderCo) focused on helping others avoid the same pitfalls.

This book is born out of my personal journey and professional mission: to help individuals, teams, and companies reclaim their workday and increase productivity without sacrificing their health. What if you could leverage productivity and focus to have peaceful evenings, consistently exercise, spend more time with your kids and family, avoid burnout, and feel better?

Over the years, I've worked with countless organizations— from tech startups to Fortune 500 companies—and the patterns are clear. High turnover rates, declining productivity, and increasing stress levels are common across multiple sectors.

Several industries are notorious for low productivity and high burnout, often stemming from systemic problems like toxic workplace cultures, high-pressure environments, and poor management practices. Clinical research, pharma, and

---

[4] "Workplace Burnout Survey," Deloitte, 2018 (https://www2.deloitte. com/us/en/pages/about-deloitte/articles/burnout-survey.html)

biotech companies, where I spent 14 years early in my career, are frequently cited for their high-stress environments. The pressure to innovate quickly can lead to long working hours without sufficient breaks. This culture of constant hustle not only burns out employees but also results in high turnover and dissatisfaction.

The finance sector paints a similar picture. The relentless demand for high performance, coupled with long hours, creates a breeding ground for mental and physical exhaustion. Employees in this industry often find themselves in a cycle of stress and fatigue, with little room for recovery.

After a period of higher-than-average turnover, Jason Deshayes, CEO at Cook Wealth, reached out to RaderCo. As a wealth management firm with 25 employees, Cook Wealth had historically invested in personal development for individual employees. Yet, they wanted an option with a broader and longer-lasting reach. We helped the team avoid the typical burnout patterns often seen in financial firms. You'll see quotes from them throughout the book.

In addition, many start-ups still operate under the romantic notion of putting in the hours, sleeping at the office, and working in "survival mode." Start-up teams desperately need productivity training that isn't steeped in "hustle culture." Too many start-up founders still believe that they and their people must suffer or be "hungry" to be competitive and successful.

Looking beyond particular industries, even when policy changes address many of the most unreasonable expectations, there can still be problems. Toxic workplace behaviors— such as unfair treatment, lack of inclusivity, and abusive management—are another major contributor to burnout across various industries. Companies that fail to address these issues face significant productivity losses and high turnover rates as employees disengage and ultimately leave.

These challenges are often exacerbated by a disconnect between employee needs and employer perceptions. Inadequate support systems and insufficient investment in mental health resources further compound the problem. However, these systemic issues are not insurmountable. Addressing them requires comprehensive strategies to improve workplace culture, provide better employee support, and create environments that promote well-being and engagement.

While all of this may feel daunting, there's good news. These issues can be transformed into opportunities for growth and success. This book offers practical, actionable solutions I've developed and refined through years of experience. You'll learn how to build a culture of productivity where employees are engaged, energized, and excited to contribute.

In these pages, you'll find:

- **Proven techniques** to enhance focus and attention that don't require a zen-like atmosphere or an unrealistic digital detox.
- **Strategies** for effective communication, even when your inbox and message app feel like a firehose.
- **Frameworks** for managing projects, tasks, and time in a way that gives you energy even when you're running on fumes.

- **Insights** into leading remote teams, promoting work-life sanity for every level of your organization, and cultivating healthy habits.

The benefits of implementing these strategies are profound. Companies that get this right see increased productivity, reduced turnover, and a happier, healthier workforce. My promise to you is that if you apply the principles in this book, you will not only improve your productivity but also create a workplace that people love to be part of.

> *"Marcey Rader has a wealth of knowledge on productivity and developing systems to improve your business flow. I've been in business for over a decade and learned great ideas I'm implementing immediately." – Dr. Amy Climer, Climer Consulting*

How to Use This Book

I've written this book to be used the same way I ask attendees in my keynotes or workshops to put ideas into action. Think of it like a buffet. Most people will not eat every single thing available at a buffet. In the same way, I don't expect you to put everything I share here into practice. Some people are allergic to items on the buffet table. You may be "allergic" to something I say. It may be that you don't want to do it or can't because of your role. You can opt to skip it and move to the next dish. That doesn't mean someone else won't love it. Lastly, there may be something on that buffet table that you make at home, but I use a different spice. There could be a behavior I suggest that you are already doing or a policy already in place at your company, and you want to tweak it just a bit. All of these are valid ways to eat at a buffet and use this book.

Here's how I recommend you approach the buffet that is *Reclaim Your Workday.*

Start with your pain points: Identify the chapters that address your most pressing challenges. Whether it's managing distractions, improving team communication, or reducing burnout, jump straight to the sections that resonate most with your current needs.

Don't skip the fundamentals: Even as you start with the chapters that address your pain points, return to Chapter 1 if you skip it. While diving into the tactics is tempting, understanding the foundational principles shared in Chapter 1 will give you a solid base. Also, each chapter starts with an introduction to the key concepts. It may be tempting to skip these introductory bits, but they provide important context. Understanding the fundamentals will make the tactics and strategies more effective when you implement them.

Apply as you go: This book is designed to be practical and actionable. As you read, start implementing the strategies right away. There's no reason to read from cover to cover before making changes. Each chapter includes actionable steps—put them into practice immediately to see results faster.

Leverage the tools: Throughout the book, you'll find references to tools, frameworks, and resources. Don't just read about them—use them. These are designed to streamline your workflow and help you stay on track.

Reflect and revisit: Productivity isn't a one-time fix. These techniques, strategies, frameworks, and insights are designed to be sustainable, meaning they will only work if you consider them part of your long-term plan. As your needs evolve, revisit different chapters. What worked for you today might need tweaking tomorrow. This book is a resource you can return to as your challenges change.

Tailor it to your role: Whether you're an individual contributor, manager, C-suite leader, or business owner, the strategies here are adaptable. Pay special attention to each chapter's "Levels" sections that offer customized advice based on your role. Also, there are good reasons you may want to read the sections that *don't* pertain to your role. For example, as a manager, you may want to read the tips for C+/Business Owners to be ready for your next climb up the ladder.

Engage with your team: If you're in a leadership position, consider reading this book with your team. Discuss the strategies together and agree on how you'll implement them company-wide. This shared understanding can amplify the benefits across your organization.

Putting it all together: Chapter 8 gives you a chance to reflect on what you read and make an action plan. If you want to get a head start on this process, note your top three takeaways as you read the previous chapters.

For example:

- Meetings: Set up my virtual workspace to be comfortable and professional on camera
- Focus and Attention: Schedule Design Days with my team for next quarter
- Healthy Habits: Take at least three screen-free lunches each week

Your next step: This book is a starting point. As you work through the chapters, think about the bigger picture. How can these strategies improve your productivity and enhance your team's efficiency and your company's culture? If you're ready to go deeper, the *Next Steps* section offers additional ways to partner with RaderCo.

Discussion questions: Reading this book with a team, book club, or group of productivity-minded friends? Check out the discussion questions at the end to help you reflect together and make sustainable changes that will help you reclaim your workday and boost productivity. For additional help shaping your policies and changing your behaviors, check out *Reclaim Your Workday Live* to guide your company through the chapters with a RaderCo Coach.

Too Long; Didn't Read (TL;DR): At the end of each section, I provide a TL;DR or brief one-paragraph summary for those who want to focus on different sections or other challenges. This will also help you focus on the strategies and frameworks that are most important to you.

Quotes and Testimonials: Throughout the book, you'll see quotes from RaderCo Team Specialists that give you additional tips. These offer a different perspective on the topic being discussed. You'll also find testimonials from RaderCo clients on what's worked for them and to guide you to figure out what sections are most pertinent. You can consider these as buffet recommendations from your favorite foodie best friend.

Don't wait for burnout to strike before making a change. The cost of inaction is too high. Turn the page to improve workplace culture, provide better employee support, and create environments that promote well-being and engagement.

CHAPTER 1

FOCUS AND ATTENTION

Maintaining focus can feel like an uphill battle in a world brimming with constant notifications, buzzing devices, and endless information. However, our ability to concentrate is not just a nice-to-have skill; it's essential for productivity and overall well-being.

Switchtasking, or attempting to juggle multiple tasks simultaneously, often masquerades as a sign of efficiency. In reality, it's a surefire route to burnout and diminished performance. Each time we switch from one task to another, our brain needs time to adjust, resulting in a loss of momentum and increased errors.[5] This cognitive "switch cost"[6] can derail even the most well-intentioned plans.

---

[5] "Why Multitasking Doesn't Work," Cleveland Clinic, March 10, 2021 (https://health.clevelandclinic.org/science-clear-multitasking-doesnt-work)

[6] Kevin P. Madore, PhD and Anthony D. Wagner, PhD, "Multicosts of Multitasking," Cerebrum, April 1, 2019 (https://www.ncbi.nlm.nih.gov/pmc/articles/PMC7075496/)

Distractions compound the problem. Every ring, ping, buzz, pop-up, and haptic drags our attention away from what truly matters, making it harder to return to the task at hand. Numerous studies have debunked the myth of multitasking, showing that our brains are wired for deep, focused work—not for hopping between tasks.[7]

At many companies, meetings throughout the day give us only 15-30 minute chunks to think, not enough time to get into a creative or deep thought zone. We check off the quick tasks, like responding to emails or instant messages, rather than doing what would actually move the needle.

All of these notifications or interruptions are microstressors. According to Rob Cross and Karen Dillon, authors of *The Microstress Effect: How Little Things Pile Up and Create Big Problems– and What To Do About Them*,[8] microstress is tiny moments of stress triggered by people in our personal and professional lives—stresses so routine that we barely register them, but whose cumulative toll is debilitating. They add up in the same way that water splashing against a pier will eventually

---

[7] Karen L. Pace, "The Myth of Multitasking: Research Say It Makes Us Less Productive and Increases Mistakes," Michigan State University, March 31, 2017 (https://www.canr.msu.edu/news/the_myth_of_multitasking_research_says_it_makes_us_less_productive_and_incr)

[8] Rob Cross and Karen Dillon, The Microstress Effect: How Little Things Pile Up and Create Big Problems–and What To Do About Them, Harvard Business Publishing, 2023 (https://store.hbr.org/product/the-microstress-effect-how-little-things-pile-up-and-create-big-problems-and-what-to-do-about-it/10573?srsltid=AfmBOooFYIaa8DI44XG1MyZ50sMyoAdI1Fm6LCVoiquvdV9xA70zUkNJ)

erode it. Our brain anticipates these stressors and can never fully relax. Our slightly elevated blood pressure becomes just a little more elevated until it's our new normal, and then more elevated. It's our newer normal, and the next thing we know... we have high blood pressure, and it feels like it happened overnight.

Types of Attention

It's essential to understand why we do the things we do, even when they are self-defeating. Why do we lose focus and how can we shift toward giving attention to the tasks that matter the most?

Human brains have two kinds of attention: involuntary and voluntary. Involuntary attention is out of our control, triggered by outside stimuli, and used for survival. It's vital if you're trying to run from an avalanche, but our brains have difficulty determining that the phone ringing, pinging, or buzzing isn't an avalanche. These interruptions still take our minds out of focus mode. Almost all individuals have a hard time ignoring loud noises and flashing lights. This could be dogs barking, airplane noise, or a cell phone ringing in the background. All these beeps, boops, and vibrations can cause microstressors we don't even realize are bothering us.

Voluntary attention is the ability to willfully focus on a task— like me writing this book or you reading it. While reading this book, have you put it down three times in the last 15 minutes to check something on the computer, get something to drink, or answer a message? As we continuously undergo interruptions, effortful control—the part of the brain that regulates attention—declines. The more you check your messages, the more you feel the need to check them, which becomes a compulsion.

> "The most helpful way I have found to foster improved focus and productivity is to help people become 'observers of their own lives'. If they still need to make a plan or schedule, I start by having them write down their activities and how long each took. The key skill is observation. Taking time to reflect on what they just did in the last half hour or hour will help them see how long various tasks take and help them plan to do similar tasks in the future. Procrastination is often a response to not knowing what can be accomplished in a set block of time. Once they begin to see how long activities take, they are more likely to see them as items that can be planned and assigned to a time on the calendar."
> – Judith Guertin, RaderCo Productivity Specialist

The Multitasking Myth

Did you know the term multitasking was never meant for humans? Multitasking was coined in 1965 in an IBM report to describe what computers are capable of that we are not—doing two or more things simultaneously. It was never meant to be a goal but to describe a machine. Our brains aren't machines. It's probably apparent that when we multitask, we're not absorbing as much as when we are focused, yet we still do it. Less is learned and even less is retrievable by the brain when taking in information while multitasking. Tasks requiring more attention, like complex exercises or numbers and formulas, are even more adversely affected by multitasking.

The hippocampus, a small structure deep in the brain's center, manages demanding cognitive tasks and creates long-term memories. The hippocampus is critical for declarative memory. When you are multitasking or distracted, the hippocampus kicks jobs down to the striatum, which handles more mundane tasks.

When you're multitasking, the mundane part of your brain may be replying to the question on the conference call or writing a response in an email because the hippocampus can't do two things at once. The striatum is the brain's autopilot. Do you want your autopilot to send your client an email?

Multitasking is not a behavior of the high performer. Science proves it's a sign of distraction. For example, if a person is trying to read an email while talking on the phone, the brain is trying to perform two language tasks that have to go through the same cognitive channel. This means that the person's mind has to go back and forth between tasks, slowing it down. As an analogy, imagine what happens when one lane on a two-way road is closed. Cars heading in one direction line up, waiting for a string of cars heading in the opposite direction to go through, then they switch. The same thing happens in a multitasking brain.

- In a study at the University of Minnesota, test workers who switchtasked or multitasked took 3-27% more time to complete reading, counting, or math problems. The more complex the interrupted task, the harder it was to get back on track.[9]

- A Microsoft study from the University of Illinois found that it takes the typical worker 15 minutes to refocus on a serious mental task after an interruption, such as responding to an incoming email or instant message. After the pause, it was also easier for them to stray and browse personal websites.[10]

- Digital distraction researcher Gloria Mark at the University of California, Irvine discovered that it takes an average of 25 minutes for the focus to return to the original task after an interruption.[11]

"How is your ability to multitask?" is a popular interview question. A trainee told me they lied during an interview and said it was "great," but in reality, they knew that multitasking decreased productivity and tried to avoid it. They thought twice about taking the job at that company after learning it was so important that it was an interview question. I work with many Human Resources professionals, and I tell them if the company job description still lists multitasking as a skill requirement, take it out or risk looking completely outdated.

---

[9] "Multitasking: Switching Costs," American Psychological Association, March 20, 2006 (https://www.apa.org/topics/research/multitasking)

[10] Steve Lohr, "A Warning on the Limits of Multitasking," New York Times, March 25, 2007 (https://www.nytimes.com/2007/03/25/business/worldbusiness/25iht-multi.1.5014965.html)

[11] Gloria Marks, Daniela Gudith, and Ulrich Klocke, "The Cost of Interrupted Work: More Speed and Stress," (https://ics.uci.edu/~gmark/chi08-mark.pdf)

You can also consider how your attention shifts when driving down the highway. Imagine a frequent drive you take. If you leave at 5:00 a.m., you're cruising at 70 miles per hour and get great gas mileage. You can get so "in the zone" you don't even have to think about driving. Compare that to rush hour, when you never get up to 70. You're constantly starting and stopping, speeding up and slowing down. Your gas mileage is awful. It costs you more money, and you're tired when you reach the destination. Multitasking feels the same.

In this chapter, you'll learn strategies to combat distractions and enhance your ability to concentrate. To be responsive instead of reactive. To play offense instead of defense. By understanding the true impact of switchtasking and the importance of establishing deep work blocks, we can reclaim our time and reduce overwhelm. We can feel accomplished at the end of the day instead of, "I worked all day and I don't know what I did."

Too Long; Didn't Read (TL;DR)

Maintaining focus today is tough. Constant notifications and information overload distract us, lowering productivity and well-being. Continue reading for strategies to increase focus and attention.

Problems:

- **Distractions:** Every ping and pop-up breaks our concentration, making it hard to get back on track.
- **Switchtasking:** Trying to juggle tasks isn't efficient. Each switch costs time and increases errors.

- **Meeting Overload:** Meetings scheduled throughout the day leave little time for deep, focused work, creativity, and problem-solving.

Solutions:

- **Efficient device set-up:** Mitigate digital distractions by turning most or all notifications off.

- **Unplug:** Discourage an always-on culture and expectations of reactivity.

- **Respect focus time:** Allow for periods of deep, focused work daily.

Levels

Action Steps for Individuals:
- Turn Off (Most) Notifications and Badges
- Turn On Do Not Disturb (DND)
- Work Offline or Pause the Inbox

Action Steps for Managers:
- Say "No" to Being Siri and Alexa
- Set Office Hours

Action Steps for C+/Business Owners:
- Say "No" to Always-On Cultures
- Implement Design Days , Focus Days, Innovation Days or Think Weeks

INDIVIDUAL

Turn Off (Most) Notifications and Badges

Turning off your notifications can help you reclaim your workday by putting you back in control and playing offense instead of defense. You can get things done faster and more effectively because you aren't losing focus each time a notification pops up on one of your devices.

> **Little known fact:** pop-ups and banners aren't on as the default to enhance your productivity. They are on to get you to use the tool, app, or program more! Those notifications are designed to be addictive because they trigger a dopamine release in the brain. Our brains get used to anticipating and wanting more of this dopamine hit.

When we get interrupted, it causes stress, frustration, and increased time pressure. If we pause what we're doing to address the interruption, we risk getting pulled in a totally different direction. Even if we get back to the original task relatively quickly, we have to refocus on where we left off, and we may feel the need to work faster to compensate for the lost time. The pressure and need to increase speed can sometimes result in mistakes.

One of the first things we do at RaderCo with coaching clients is disable any pop-up or banner notifications on their phones and computers that aren't necessary to them. Yes, even email notifications! Email is needed, but for most people, reacting as soon as an email arrives is not the best use of their time.

Notifications create reactivity instead of responsiveness. We need to prioritize to respond to emails and other work requests effectively. We never have time to focus when we are continually alerted to this and that and who and what. Each request feels urgent, so we react with urgency. Then, what's worse, we teach people that we are reactors, which becomes an expectation. Suddenly, we live by their timelines and rules rather than our own. *Your inbox is another person's agenda.*

A response is defined as timely for your role and not done out of a false sense of urgency or time pressure.

Note: If your job requires reactivity (e.g., help desks or customer service), this may be an item on the behavior menu that you have an allergy to, but you could turn off other notifications, like social media, ESPN, or the Weather Channel, that do not require your reactive attention.

Also, if you think you can tune out notifications, you're wrong. It affects everyone to varying degrees. People often tell me, "When I get a notification, I just ignore it." Well, the very fact that you knew you got one means that you didn't actually ignore it. Notifications trigger the involuntary part of your brain. You can't help it. They also elicit a dopamine response, which is the same one you get from gambling and other potentially addictive behaviors.

The default for most email and chat tools is to have pop-ups, banners, noises, badges, etc., all on. Sometimes, you'll even get an *email* telling you that you have a chat message! Instead, turn *off* as many as you can. I've yet to have someone forget to process their email or tend to their chats (unless they read them and postpone answering, trying to remember to go back to them later). I've also never had anyone lose their job because they turned off their notifications. The overwhelming majority of people state that it has been a "lifesaver," a "gamechanger," and "less stressful."

If you feel nervous about it, start with one device. One of the questions I ask in our RaderCo training is, "How many devices do your email or chat notifications come in on?" People regularly respond with two, three, or as many as five different devices! This probably means a laptop, phone, tablet, watch, and another device...maybe a home computer or second phone. That is a lot of extra swipes that are unnecessary throughout the day.

I don't get any email notifications, nor does anything come to my email to notify me I have a message, e.g., LinkedIn or ClickUp, our project management system (PMS). I'm on LinkedIn once or twice a day, and I have my PMS open all day, so I don't need an extra notification.

Badges are the little number or bubble on your phone that tells you that you have something waiting for you. For most people, this number calls to them, and since we're curious people, we have to see what's waiting for us. Some of us will even tap the message to get that badge down to zero, knowing full well that we'll have to go back and re-read the message later.

I keep my badge on for voice mail because hardly anyone calls me, and it has more of a sense of urgency. Your experience may be different. You may get a lot of phone calls. I also have a badge for Voxer, the walkie-talkie app we use for RaderCo, because that's how I communicate with my Team Specialists. Still, that app goes into *Do Not Disturb* mode during off-work hours, and I never have banners or sounds on.

TL;DR

Turn off your email, instant message, or any other program pop-ups, banners, or badges.

Turn On Do Not Disturb

My phone is in *Do Not Disturb* (DND) mode almost all day because I'm either doing focused work, meeting with a coaching client, or giving a virtual presentation. If I'm expecting a call, I'll turn DND off. Fortunately, in my business, most people set up an appointment before calling me and don't just ring me out of the blue, but if they do call, they can always leave me a voicemail. Having DND on also keeps me from getting interrupted by telemarketers or robocalls (by the Power of Grayskull, can someone please stop this?).

If, unlike me, you have a business or job where you need to have your phone on, think about a time of day when you need to have focus or quiet time and turn on DND for 30 to 60 minutes. Create guardrails for your morning or evening when you want to focus on yourself or your family. I have an automatic DND on my phone from 8:00 p.m. to 8:00 a.m. This means only calls or texts from people on my *Favorites* list get through to me. I must intentionally look at my phone to see a text or voicemail. In the morning, I'm not looking at texts first thing, getting interrupted by a ping during my workout or while meditating, or distracted during my first 90-minute work sprint, which is my most productive time. My friends know if they text me in the morning, it won't bother me because my phone is in DND. I'll look at it when I'm ready.

You get to determine who you want to be on your *Favorites* list. Maybe it's your immediate family, boss, top client, and best friend. Perhaps it's NOT your family (because they text you all day long), and maybe you don't want your top client to have that much access to you. Perhaps it's just the school that your kids attend. Create blocks for DND throughout your day and go one step further by *automating* when your phone goes into that mode and scheduling it in your settings.

TL;DR

Create an automatic Do Not Disturb (DND) time in your phone settings.

Work Offline or Pause the Inbox

Working offline is a productivity hack that prevents you from getting distracted by emails that continue to arrive in your inbox when you're processing what's already there. It allows you to catch up, retrieve emails you need for what you're currently working on, decrease inappropriate responses, or accidentally send something too quickly, and it just plain saves time.

Selecting *Work Offline* in Outlook means no new emails will come in, and emails you compose will sit in the *outbox* until you go back online. This is a great feature if you are working off-hours and don't want to schedule each email individually to be sent during work hours or don't want people to know you are working.

You can *pause* your inbox using the Boomerang extension (also available for Outlook) in Gmail. You can send emails anytime (they don't sit in your outbox), but you don't see new ones unless you *unpause* them. A feature also allows you to unpause automatically at certain times of the day. I use this feature and unpause twice daily, and no one has ever said I didn't respond fast enough. Another helpful feature is that you can put specific email addresses, domain names, or words on an *allowed* list, and those emails never get paused. Examples of mine are anything from Dropbox Sign or DocuSign (because these are contracts), my CFO and accountant, my largest client, and anyone who has hired me to speak in the few days preceding the event.

> "I'm using Inbox Pause, and I'm actually surprised by what a big difference it made—immediately. My brain is less crazy." – Sara R. Shelp, CPA

Working offline and waiting to respond to emails immediately changes the conversation. Have you noticed that when you reply (aka react) right away, and the recipient realizes you are online, a discussion develops back and forth? Email starts to become like an instant messaging program, and you feel rude if you don't reply immediately because they know you are online.

What About Instant Messaging and Chat?

I really wish they wouldn't have called this "instant" because people mistakenly thought this meant they needed to reply instantly. It's now more often referred to as chat. For the love of kittens, do not keep your chat window up all day long. This results in continuous partial attention or never fully being focused. If you work in an industry where the culture is more messaging-heavy than email-heavy (like tech) and you can't imagine closing the window all day, what about not having it open for the first and last 30-60 minutes of your day, so that time is yours to work on top tasks or close things out? Or what if you only had your chat tool open for two to three hours daily instead?

Use the *Do Not Disturb* mode for deep work time, but go one step further. In your *status message*, state that you are "focusing," "concentrating," "in mission-critical mode," or whatever it is you want to call it, and then put the time you will be online again. This reduces the anxiety some people may feel about when you will be available. I *do not* recommend putting an out-of-office message in your email that will tell people when you will be checking your email. That's just an annoying email that people will have to delete. Most people don't expect urgent responses or care what time you read them.

And….please don't think, type, and hit *enter* one line at a time in your chats. Just because it's quick doesn't mean you word-vomit sentence by sentence. Think about what you want to say. Write all of it. Then hit send.

Also, please don't send a chat or text that just says, "Hey," "Hi," or "Can I ask you a question?" It's a waste of a message, and now I have to reply and ask what you need (or most likely, I'll just ignore it until you send a follow-up). Please tell me in the original message.

TL;DR

Work offline or paused during times of focused work, or at least for a 30-minute burst daily. Use a status message in your chat tool to state that you are in focus mode and when you will be available next.

MANAGER

Say No to Being "Siri" and "Alexa"

Do you feel like your first name has become Siri, Alexa, Echo, or Hey Google? Many leaders feel like they need to be always available, but have you ever considered that this could stunt the growth of your team? If they never need to figure out something independently, they aren't being pushed to solve problems. If they see that you are always available, they don't feel empowered to block time for deep work themselves. You are modeling the behavior and expectations for your team.

Many of our clients in leadership roles do their "real" work at night because they are interrupted so much during the day. I'd argue that managing is real work, but they mean they are being interrupted so much that they can't do *focused* work. That's because they are taking on the role of Siri or Alexa for their teams, and they can change this by implementing office hours.

Be accessible when it makes sense and not all the time.

Yes, managers need to be accessible, but supporting your team doesn't mean being available at all hours to answer every one of their questions immediately. If you react to every request, you are not allowing them to think through it themselves. You are creating a culture that lacks research and resources...*self-directed resources.* It also means you aren't giving yourself the dedicated time for strategy, creativity, and planning, which require uninterrupted sacred time.

Many countries around the world understand this and have gone so far as to enact legislation guaranteeing a "right to disconnect" outside of work hours. More than one dozen countries have approved some version of this law, with France being the first in 2017 and Australia being the most recent in February 2024. This law hasn't made it to the U.S. just yet, though a San Francisco Assemblyman did introduce legislation that was inspired by Australia's policy that wouldn't allow workers to be penalized for not answering an email or text during off-hours (dependent on role).[12]

And in case you think this is a passing fad, Raven Solomon, an expert on Intergenerational Differences, and Justin Jones-Fosu, an expert on Workplace Engagement, shared a shocking trend. Many in the Gen Z age group look less at leadership roles as the path to success and want to remain individual

---

[12]   Rachel Treisman, "Australia is the latest country to give workers a 'right to disconnect' after hours," NPR, August 26, 2024 (https://www.npr.org/2024/08/26/nx-s1-5089792/australia-right-to-disconnect-workers-respond-after-work?utm_source=npr_newsletter&utm_medium=email&utm_content=20240827&utm_term=9674525&utm_campaign=news&utm_id=64460031&orgid=&utm_att1=)

contributors! They are seeing the lives of Boomers and Gen Xers and don't want that always-on, burned-out, glazed look in their eyes. They want to take vacations without the expectation of plugging in or being available. We must turn this tide quickly, or we will be hurting for strong leaders in about a decade.

"As Born Digital, GenZ are bombarded with exponentially more information and stimuli than generations before us. The external pressure to prove ourselves at the workplace creates even more mental clutter, making it difficult for us to find the mental space needed for creativity and sustained attention." – Rijul Arora, RaderCo Digital Wellness and Microsoft Specialist

Do you think that if you say, "Just because I work at night or weekends, I don't expect you to," your team won't feel pressured to check "just in case?" Wrong. If you are in a position of authority, know that most people who work for you will feel compelled to check if they know you work on the weekends.

A friend in a high-level position at a major pharmaceutical company told me a story about the new CEO who said she liked to work on weekends but didn't expect others to. Because the CEO didn't schedule her emails during working hours (Mistake #1), she sent an email to five people in high-level positions around noon on a Sunday, including my friend. Within an hour, all of them had responded. My friend was the last one. She was at a family picnic and checked her email (mistake #2), and because everyone else had responded, she felt like she had to. She kicked herself for giving in but said she couldn't help herself. She didn't want to look like the one person who wasn't dedicated!

TL;DR

Refrain from being always available and allow yourself to work in focused blocks. Schedule emails to send during work hours since being in a position of authority can put your team members into "just in case" mode.

Use status messages in your chat tool and indicate when you are available for questions.

Set Office Hours

Think about your professor in college who had open office hours. Those were the only times you could stop by their office. The hours were specified, and you saved up your questions until they were available. I'm not suggesting you should only be open two to three times a week, but what if you had 30 minutes in the morning or afternoon when you signed on to Zoom or Teams? What if you reserved one hour once or twice weekly for specific questions? Anyone who had a question could pop in and ask you then, instead of being disruptive during your planning time by sending you a chat or message.

You simply keep people in the waiting room until it's their turn. While they're waiting, they can be working. Then, when you're ready, you let them in and answer their question. You can choose to have people sign up, but just letting people in as you finish with someone else is more efficient. All you have to do is create a standing link at a specific time, and people will know how to get to you. If no one joins your office hours, you can still be working while waiting; you just have your video on while doing it.

Video Office Hour Wins

- You aren't interrupted throughout the day.
- Your people know when they can reach you and may research their questions themselves.
- Everyone gets to the point because the time is limited, and people may be in line in the waiting room.
- There isn't a back-and-forth email chain. It's a "get to the facts" direct session.

You could implement this type of meeting in multiple ways. I use it for an Ask the Expert (helloraderco.com/ask-the-expert) session 30-45 days after giving a training. I hang out on Zoom for 25 minutes. Anyone attending the workshop can join and ask me questions about what they learned, share a new habit, or share a challenge they need help solving. For Ask the Expert sessions, I don't keep people in a waiting room because others may have the same question.

Many group coaches also use this format. I worked with a book coach while writing this book. He has office hours twice a week for one hour. If I have a question, I sign on and just wait until he lets me in. I can be in and out in less than a couple of minutes, or it could take up to ten, depending on what I need and how many others are waiting to talk to him. It's not wasted time because I'm working while waiting for him.

Regular video hours could also be used for customer support or training calls. Depending on your volume, they could be daily, weekly, or monthly.

You can also do this in person. My client, Jim West, has "open office hours" every day from 4:15 p.m. to 5:15 p.m., during which people can come by his desk and ask him anything. He knows not to schedule focused work during that time, and his team will save up any questions and ask him during that time.

If you're often asked for brain-picking sessions, direct people to sign up and make it a group session so everyone can learn. A former female CEO coaching client was in high demand by young women to mentor them. She wanted to do it but needed help prioritizing her time to invest in it. Instead of meeting with them individually, I recommended she choose a time she would be at a coffee shop for an hour once per month or quarter and tell people they could join her there and ask her anything.

TL;DR

Depending on your role, use video or in-person office hours one to two times per week, or even daily, to make it easy to schedule time to support your team and for them to know when they can get their questions answered.

C+/BUSINESS OWNER

Say "No" to Always-On Cultures

A reactive culture always expects workers to be available. Some companies will *say* people don't need to be reactive or always on. Still, actions demonstrating otherwise—working during vacations, not giving people focused work time, requiring responses immediately or urgently even when things aren't urgent—can undermine productivity and harm the health of your staff.

Always-on cultures contribute significantly to burnout since burnout tends not to come from our workload but from what we're *not doing outside of work* to recharge our energy batteries. Constant connectivity can lead to mental fatigue, and distractions lead to more mistakes and lower-quality output. Creativity and innovation are stifled without the mental space or downtime that people need. A lack of guardrails between work and personal life can lead to higher stress levels, even for team members' families. The anticipatory stress of mom, dad, or partner/spouse getting a text or email that will take them away from family time, dinner, or upset their mood is a microstress for the family as well. Ultimately, it can lead to employee turnover or disinterest in leadership roles.

> *"The constant pressure to always be available or 'always on' takes a serious toll on both mental and physical health. It leads to burnout, stifles creativity, and causes people to feel disconnected, as they go through the motions without a real break. Over time, this nonstop demand drains people, negatively affecting their personal lives, health, and happiness.*

Further, organizations are losing productivity and profitability as their employees struggle to navigate the new world of work." – Dawn Sander, RaderCo Leadership and Strengths Specialist

To deal with this problem, 12 countries, mainly in Europe and South America, have gone so far as to enact legislation protecting a worker's "right to disconnect" outside of work hours. Here in the U.S., there are signs that some states might be considering moving in this direction. Legislation proposed by Assemblyman Matt Haney in California would give workers the legal right to ignore non-emergency calls and emails once the workday ends without being penalized for future advancement or promotion.[13]

This may be one of those places where you feel allergic to my recommendation. Keep in mind that there can be exceptions to the rule that don't necessarily lead to burnout. If something is mission-critical *and* time-sensitive—for example, a launch in a different time zone or an audit—then it may be appropriate for employees to be ready to respond outside of work hours. What's important is that after the urgency passes, everyone goes back to maintaining guardrails.

As a biotech company working to advance a deep pipeline of precision therapies that are designed to improve patients' lives, RaderCo client Blueprint Medicines had no shortage of smart

---

[13] Morgan Smith, "Your boss could be fined $100 for bothering you after work under a newly proposed California law," CNBC, April 11, 2014 (https://www.cnbc.com/2024/04/11/california-proposed-right-to-disconnect-law-would-fine-companies-for-after-hours-communication.html)

and talented employees who were extremely passionate about their work. Yet, because of the company's fast-paced industry, rapid growth, and commitment to delivering life-saving medicines, that passion often propelled their lean "Blue Crew" to put work first—sometimes sacrificing work-life balance and personal priorities. You'll hear more about Blueprint Medicines' implementation of sustainable productivity strategies and see quotes from their team throughout the book.

> *"RaderCo helped our employees feel more in control and realize they could do many things they thought they couldn't do, like manage their calendars, set boundaries around their time, and disconnect on weekends and vacations." – Jen Shevlin, Vice President of Human Resources, Blueprint Medicines*

Evaluate Communication Expectations

Create a culture where people *who take real, unplugged vacations are rewarded,* rather than those who make themselves available during time with their family or their cruise at sea. Emphasize the importance of taking mental breaks during off-hours.

The messaging platform Slack is often antithetic to productivity, but not the way the company Slack uses it! They encourage using DND mode and for employees to disconnect outside of work hours (and mean it). They even have a giant sign in their office that says, "Work Hard and Go Home." They don't log on at home; sending a message after hours is considered rude.

Even the Chief Revenue and Chief Marketing Officer schedules time to go into Slack to read messages and then *closes it out.*[14]

TL;DR

Create a culture that respects guardrails off-hours, unless something mission-critical is also time-sensitive (such as undergoing an audit or launch). Implore management and leadership to set an example by not sending emails or chats off-hours (people can work if they wish, but schedule to send later).

Implement Design Days, Focus Days, Innovation Days, Think Weeks

Design Days, Focus Days, Innovation Days, Think Weeks… there are many names to call this time. Whatever you opt for, it's one of the most important things a company and an individual can implement throughout their work year. We are so bogged down in tasks and "stuff" that we don't give ourselves time to think and be creative.

Problem-solving and innovation cannot occur during 15-minute increments between 30-minute meetings or while answering emails or chats.

Our work volume is higher than it has ever been. The search term *"How to Focus at Work"* increased 300% in 2023! We are a nation of over-communicators, and working remotely is

---

[14] Nir Eyal, "If Tech is so Distracting, How Do Slack Employees Stay Focused?" Bonusly, January 16, 2020 (https://bonusly.com/post/slack-employees-stay-focused)

being felt with even more disruption due to those automatic notifications.

One answer to this is Design Days (helloraderco.com/design-days). RaderCo's definition is one full day or more with no meetings, email, text, or chat messages, and completely open to solve problems, create, and thinkitate. It's a day dedicated to focus time that can be used for reflection, planning, mind mapping, training, or just finishing that project.

During a Design Day, we can complete the things we often don't have time for or that get pushed to the back burner. We can work on those things that we know are value-added but sit in the "parking lot" for weeks or months because we can't carve out time for them. It can open up space for learning and training to enable career progression.

My clients and I have used Design Days to invent a new concept, work through a bottleneck, or design a new service or product.

We've used them for organization and planning, especially at the end of the year when we're working through our Powered Path Playbook® (helloraderco.com/playbook) and doing our reflections.

Our coaching clients often complain about wanting to learn more about the company and their industry or work on their personal and professional development but needing more time to do so. Design Days can be used for training, increasing brand knowledge, or research.

Bill Gates called this time Think Week. He would take one week, twice yearly, away from tech and society, go to a cabin in the woods, and read.

Justin Jones-Fosu, founder of Work Meaningful, takes Think Weeks or Think Weekends each quarter to reflect, plan, and work on new offerings or write new content.

Why not extend this to your entire company?

My client Abdo, an accounting and advisory firm with over 200 employees, has two Focus Weeks yearly. For a whole week, there are no internal meetings. It's time to do deep work without interruption. Some Abdo employees choose to vacation during this time since they know they won't be returning to an overflowing inbox or tasks from meetings they missed. Still, a holiday without work stress can also be a great way to come up with solutions. The initiative aims to boost productivity and give employees dedicated time to work on complex tasks without distractions. They also have Focus Fridays, where they don't schedule meetings on Fridays.

RaderCo partnered with biotech company Blueprint Medicines, with over 600 employees globally, to implement company-wide Design Days three times a year, and it has been wildly successful. Most of the company shuts down their inboxes and Microsoft Teams chats for a day, and works outside the inbox. I say most because some critical staff (for example, those essential for patient safety) can't unplug; however, they have fewer or no meetings and aren't distracted by the people who have unplugged. When we were piloting Design Days, one of Blueprint Medicines' team members came up with a process he had never had time to do before. It solved a bottleneck that ultimately saved them money and time.[15] Having Design Days can also be an impressive recruitment and retention tool. Wouldn't you want to work for a company that recognizes the impact of time to be innovative?

"We hire smart, talented, and productive people, and Design Days allows them a day to reflect, think, plan, and execute without feeling bound by emails or meetings. There was nothing stopping people from taking this time before, but it's hard not to feel the organizational pressure and the self-pressure to respond to emails and be in meetings. Design Days alleviates that." – Jen Shevlin, Vice President of Human Resources, Blueprint Medicines

In the latest impact summary for Design Days at Blueprint Medicines, 90% of respondents said that it enabled them to dedicate more time to high-impact work, fostering an environment where they could open their minds to innovative thinking, solve complex problems, and brainstorm transformative possibilities. Ninety-six percent of respondents would recommend Design Days to others.

---

[15] Blueprint Medicines Case Study (www.helloraderco.com/blueprint-case-study)

One anonymous responder said, "I attended a conference in March and went to a great session, which I found really insightful. Design Day allowed me to revisit my notes and dig in deeper than I was able with my regular schedule full of many other duties. It was a great learning day and brought me back to the lab feeling more inspired than ever."

> "Neglecting to provide thinking time can stifle creativity, lead to poor decision-making, and increase stress for all employees, particularly introverts, who may feel overlooked and anxious in fast-paced environments. Cultivating a culture that values reflection not only enhances engagement and job satisfaction but also fosters a more inclusive and innovative workplace where diverse perspectives can thrive." – Dawn Sander, RaderCo Leadership and Strengths Specialist

LinkedIn staff have "InDays" once a month, during which they can focus on innovation, self-improvement, or community service away from regular work duties.

Slack is known for having "Focus Fridays," where no meetings are scheduled, allowing employees to concentrate on deep work.

Facebook implements "No Meeting Wednesdays" to provide uninterrupted time for employees to focus.

Asana has periodic "No Meeting Days" to enable team members to work on tasks uninterrupted.

My recommendation for companies to implement Design Days is to do them once per month or once per quarter and plan them out for the entire year so people don't already have meetings scheduled. Block out calendars from an *enterprise level*. Send a reminder email one to two weeks out to remind people to plan what they will work on for Design Day. That way, they will have time to reach out if they need something from someone (a report, confirmation, etc.), and they won't be scrambling to get it on Design Day when they aren't supposed to distract anyone.

I also recommend having Design Days during mid-year and annual review periods so people can focus on performance reviews instead of trying to fit them in between tasks. You could also have them before a launch, during a heavy data-driven time, or a few weeks before an annual shutdown. As a founder, I like including them at the end of the year to reflect and plan for the following year.

Planning Design Day

- As a company, do at least one per month or quarter. Schedule them for the year so people can plan.

- Block calendars at the beginning of the year or when you determine the date.

- Remind your employees one to two weeks in advance and remind them to get whatever they need before Design Day.

- Individuals can do them as often as needed, depending on their role. Some feel like quarterly is a gift, whereas others take one full day a week without meetings, emails, or chats. Be supportive of people taking individual Design Days.

During Design Day

- Empower staff to put on their out-of-office messages for clients to see that they will be offline to...create better systems and processes for clients, do deep work to innovate, or save patient lives. Get creative! Please don't be embarrassed, worried about how it will look, or feel like it should be a secret. Speaking as a client, I know I want the vendors or companies I work with to think strategically and creatively.

- Remind people the day before: *No email or instant message.* These should be closed entirely out on Design Day. If that's truly impossible, allow external communication only.

TL;DR

Schedule company-wide Design Days, Innovation Days, or Focus Weeks monthly to quarterly. Block out calendars in advance *on an enterprise level.* Buckle up for all the creative solutions and problem-solving that will happen!

References

Rob Cross and Karen Dillon, *The Microstress Effect: How Little Things Pile Up and Create Big Problems–and What To Do About Them*, Harvard Business Publishing, 2023 (https://store.hbr.org/product/the-microstress-effect-how-little-things-pile-up-and-create-big-problems-and-

what-to-do-about-it/10573?srsltid=AfmBOooFYIaa8DI
44XG1MyZ50sMyoAdI1Fm6LCVoiquvdV9xA70zUkNJ)

Nir Eyal, "If Tech is so Distracting, How Do Slack Employees
Stay Focused?" Bonusly, January 16, 2020 (https://
bonusly.com/post/slack-employees-stay-focused)

Steve Lohr, "A Warning on the Limits of Multitasking,"
New York Times, March 25, 2007 (https://
www.nytimes.com/2007/03/25/business/
worldbusiness/25iht-multi.1.5014965.html)

Kevin P. Madore, PhD and Anthony D. Wagner,
PhD, "Multicosts of Multitasking," Cerebrum,
April 1, 2019 (https://www.ncbi.nlm.nih.
gov/pmc/articles/PMC7075496/)

Gloria Marks, Daniela Gudith, and Ulrich Klocke, "The
Cost of Interrupted Work: More Speed and Stress,"
(https://ics.uci.edu/~gmark/chi08-mark.pdf)

Karen L. Pace, "The Myth of Multitasking: Research Say It
Makes Us Less Productive and Increases Mistakes,"
Michigan State University, March 31, 2017 (https://
www.canr.msu.edu/news/the_myth_of_multitasking_
research_says_it_makes_us_less_productive_and_incr)

Morgan Smith, "Your boss could be fined $100 for
bothering you after work under a newly proposed
California law," CNBC, April 11, 2014 (https://
www.cnbc.com/2024/04/11/california-proposed-
right-to-disconnect-law-would-fine-companies-
for-after-hours-communication.html)

Rachel Treisman, "Australia is the latest country to give
workers a 'right to disconnect' after hours," NPR,
August 26, 2024 (https://www.npr.org/2024/08/26/

nx-s1-5089792/australia-right-to-disconnect-workers-respond-after-work?utm_source=npr_newsletter&utm_medium=email&utm_content=20240827&utm_term=9674525&utm_campaign=news&utm_id=64460031&orgid=&utm_att1=)

Blueprint Medicines Case Study (www.helloraderco.com/blueprint-case-study)

"Multitasking: Switching Costs," American Psychological Association, March 20, 2006 (https://www.apa.org/topics/research/multitasking)

"Why Multitasking Doesn't Work," Cleveland Clinic, March 10, 2021 (https://health.clevelandclinic.org/science-clear-multitasking-doesnt-work)

CHAPTER 2

EMAIL AND CHAT MESSAGING

Now that you have some tools to increase your focus and attention and the foundation for a healthy and productive routine, we're ready to get tactical with emails and instant messaging.

> Reminder: this is a buffet. Depending on the type and size of your company, industry, and role, you may skip some recommendations and expand on others.

Remember that you have loads of resources in print, audio, and video to guide you through this process; improvement will not happen overnight.

The Double-Edged Sword of Email and Chat Tools

When interviewing for your job, did you tell them about your amazing email-checking abilities? Did you discuss your sharp skills with Teams, Slack, or Chat? Doubtful. We're being interviewed for "zone of genius" work, yet we spend most days responding and writing messages.

Email and chat tools are essential for communication, yet they are often the biggest culprits behind reduced productivity and increased stress. Microsoft Teams, Slack, Google Chat, and Cisco Webex are the most popular chat or messaging apps.

The average office worker receives 121 emails and 96 chat messages per day, according to a study by the Radicati Group.[16] This constant stream of information can lead to information overload, where employees struggle to prioritize tasks and maintain focus.

And workers check their chat tool every six minutes, according to a study by RescueTime.[17] Thinking back to Chapter 1, you realize that *no one is doing deep work* if this is the case at your workplace.

The expectation for immediate responses from chats can create a culture of constant availability, contributing to burnout and anxiety. Research by the American Psychological Association highlights that 62% of workers experience increased stress levels due to the pressure of always being "on." [18] This is even worse with employees who work remotely and feel like if they don't respond immediately, their boss and co-workers may

---

[16] "Email Statistics Report 2021-2025," Radicati Group, Inc., February 2021 (https://www.radicati.com/wp/wp-content/uploads/2020/12/Email-Statistics-Report-2021-2025-Executive-Summary.pdf)

[17] Jory MacKay, "Communication Overload: Our Research Shows Most Workers Can't Go 6 Minutes Without Checking Email or IM," RescueTime, July 11, 2018 (https://blog.rescuetime.com/communication-multitasking-switches/)

[18] "Stress in America 2020," American Psychological Association, October 1, 2020 (https://www.apa.org/news/press/releases/stress/2020/report-october)

think they are "goofing off." Why do we assume those who don't react immediately aren't working instead of the alternative, which is that they are doing deep work?

The use of additional external monitors can make this reactivity even worse. As someone who regularly works from three screens (and five when I'm presenting virtually), I know that multiple monitors can make some people less productive if they always have their email or chat open on one screen and "work" from another, for example. Instead, a better way to use multiple monitors is to have two things open that you need, like a spreadsheet on one and a report you are writing about the spreadsheet on another. Keeping email or chat open all day on one of your monitors is a surefire way to be distracted.

Companies must adopt strategic practices for managing email and chat tools to combat these challenges. Implementing guidelines for response times and determining what's truly urgent, encouraging focused work periods free from digital interruptions, and promoting a culture that values the balance between availability and deep work time can significantly enhance productivity and employee well-being.

How many of the emails you write are unnecessary? We could all reduce the number of emails we send and receive by avoiding unnecessary messages, creating better subject lines, and taking some time to write canned emails for scenarios that come up repeatedly.

This chapter discusses the top strategies I use with my clients to streamline email and chat messages so that employees can spend more time working in their zone of genius.

TL;DR

Email and chat are crucial but, when not properly prioritized, harm productivity and increase stress. Office workers get an average of 121 emails and 96 chat messages daily, leading to information overload. Workers check chat tools every six minutes on average, disrupting deep work. The pressure for instant responses fuels constant availability, causing burnout. Companies must manage email and chat tools effectively, set response guidelines, and encourage focused work periods to improve productivity and well-being.

Problems:

High Volume: An overwhelming number of emails and chat messages daily makes effective management tough.[19]

Difficulty Prioritizing: It's hard to distinguish urgent tasks, leading to poor prioritization and missed deadlines.[20]

Lack of Clarity: Frequent misunderstandings occur, requiring additional clarification and causing delays.[21]

---

[19] Hazel Emnace, "17 Business Email Statistics and Trends to Watch in 2024," Fit Small Business, November 23, 2023 (https://fitsmallbusiness.com/business-email-statistics-and-trends/)

[20] Jayson DeMers, "Email Productivity Benchmark Report (May 2023)," Email Analytics (https://emailanalytics.com/email-productivity-benchmark-report/)

[21] Radica Boshnjakoska, "How Many Emails Are Sent Per Day in 2024," Review 42, February 13, 2024 (https://review42.com/resources/how-many-emails-are-sent-per-day)

Frequent Interruptions: Constantly checking messages disrupts workflow and decreases productivity.[22] [23]

Switchtasking: Switching between tasks and platforms reduces efficiency and focus.[24] [25]

Slow Response Times: The high volume and complexity of messages lead to delayed responses that can stall projects.[26]

Multi-Platform Confusion: Managing conversations across multiple platforms fragments communication.[27]

Always-On Culture: The expectation for constant availability fuels burnout and hinders disconnection.[28]

[22] Hazel Emnace, "17 Business Email Statistics and Trends to Watch in 2024," Fit Small Business, November 23, 2023 (https://fitsmallbusiness.com/business-email-statistics-and-trends/)

[23] Jayson DeMers, "Email Productivity Benchmark Report (May 2023)," Email Analytics (https://emailanalytics.com/email-productivity-benchmark-report/)

[24] Jayson DeMers, "Email Productivity Benchmark Report (May 2023)," Email Analytics (https://emailanalytics.com/email-productivity-benchmark-report/)

[25] Radica Boshnjakoska, "How Many Emails Are Sent per Day in 2024?," Review 42, February 13, 2024 (https://review42.com/resources/how-many-emails-are-sent-per-day/)

[26] Radica Boshnjakoska, "How Many Emails Are Sent Per Day in 2024," Review 42, February 13, 2024 (https://review42.com/resources/how-many-emails-are-sent-per-day)

[27] "The Surprising Connection Between After-Hours Work and Decreased Productivity," Slack, December 5, 2023 (https://slack.com/blog/news/the-surprising-connection-between-after-hours-work-and-decreased-productivity)

[28] "The Surprising Connection Between After-Hours Work and Decreased Productivity," Slack, December 5, 2023 (https://slack.com/blog/news/the-surprising-connection-between-after-hours-work-and-decreased-productivity)

Solutions:

Inbox Categories: Separate emails into categories to distinguish important and urgent from non-urgent.

Email Filters: Use filters or rules to organize incoming emails automatically.

Templates: Create email templates to save time on routine responses.

Reply All: Establish company-wide guidelines for when to use "reply all" to avoid unnecessary emails.

To/CC Lines: To clarify responsibilities, use "To" and "CC" lines correctly and consistently.

Subject Lines: Develop naming conventions for subject lines to make searching easier.

Scheduled Delivery: Schedule or delay the delivery of emails and chat messages to avoid interruptions during off-hours.

No-Email/Chat Times: Designate specific times when email and chat are turned off to allow for focused work.

Communications Matrix: Create a matrix to determine the appropriate communication channel for different types of messages.

Project Management System: Implement a project management system to centralize tasks and communication (see Chapter 4).

Levels

Action Steps for Individuals:
- Create Inbox Categories
- Use Filters and Rules
- Develop Email Templates

Action Steps for Managers:
- Create a Policy for "Reply All"
- Implement Subject Lines and Naming Conventions
- Use Schedule Send

Action Steps for C+/Business Owners:
- Designate No-Email or Chat Times
- Develop a Communications Matrix

INDIVIDUAL

Create Inbox Categories

Inbox categories can help you prioritize by seeing the important emails separately from marketing, notifications, and updates. Think of it as an automatic filtering mechanism to save you time. The *Focused/Other* inbox in Outlook is designed to help users manage their email by automatically sorting incoming messages into two tabs: *Focused* and *Other*. The *Focused* tab contains the most important emails, such as those from frequent contacts or marked as high-priority, ensuring they get your attention first. The *Other* tab holds less critical emails, like newsletters and promotional offers.

In Gmail, you can organize by *Primary, Promotions,* and *Updates* tabs.

Primary: personal and important messages.

Promotions: marketing emails, deals, and promotional content.

Updates: notifications, receipts, bills, and statements.

For all these, you can train the system to filter emails to go into one category or another by selecting *Always Move to Focused (Outlook)* or clicking *Labels,* then selecting *Promotions/Updates, etc. (Gmail)* if they go into the wrong category. Changing these views in your settings is quick and very effective at allowing you to see your most important emails without the clutter.

Gmail has other useful features like Priority Inbox, Important First, Starred First, or Multiple Inbox view. Check out the book *Taming the Digital Tiger: A Step-by-Step Guide to Tame Your Gmail Account in No Time Flat* by Judith Guertin and Barbara Hemphill.[29]

TL;DR

For prioritized viewing, change your settings to *Focus/Other* in Outlook or *Primary/Promotions/Updates* in Gmail.

---

[29]   Judith Guertin and Barbara Hemphill, Taming the Digital Tiger: A Step-by-Step Guide to Tame Your Gmail Account in No Time Flat, Write Way Publishing Company, February 10, 2021 (https://www.abebooks.com/9781946425829/Taming-Digital-Tiger-Step-by-Step-Guide-1946425826/plp)

Use Filters and Rules

Going beyond categories, we can set up more specific filters and rules to save even more time processing emails. We get so many emails throughout the day that we often have to look through the "weeds" to see the "flowers." You may get six emails about a shipping report when you only need to see the last one. Or an email from our top client gets mixed in with the benefits email from HR. Setting up rules can make the right ones stand out to prioritize.

Creating rules or filters to organize your incoming email is game-changing! Note that in Outlook, it's called a *rule*. In Gmail, it's called a *filter*. I will refer to it as a *rule* throughout. Because the steps may differ depending on your version, I suggest searching for "how to create a rule/filter in Outlook/Gmail." Also, we have folders in Outlook, and in Gmail, we have labels. I'll refer to them as folders throughout.

Benefits:

Reduces Clutter: Automatically sorts incoming emails into folders.

Saves Time: Eliminates manual sorting and filing.

Increases Focus: Filters out less important emails so you can concentrate on high-priority messages or keep interruptions at bay.

Improves Organization: Helps categorize emails by project, client, or urgency, making it easier to find specific emails later.

You can start with a rule that a message from a specific email address gets sent to a particular folder before or after it's opened. Instead of opening and dragging an email I don't need to a folder, it automatically goes where I can choose to view it later.

Here's an example: I worked with a large auto dealership, and they received up to thirteen email reports daily about sales from one vendor, but they only needed the final report. They set up a rule for all the reports from that email address to skip the inbox and go to one *Sales Reports* folder. At the end of the day, they checked the latest report. 13 emails a day multiplied by 13 managers equals a lot of wasted emails!

Get emails even after you've unsubscribed? Create a rule that anything coming *from that domain* goes straight to the trash, so you never have to see it in your inbox.

Ideas for Rules:

- Receipts from online purchases—Nicole, an interior designer, gets an incredible number of receipts. She created a rule for anything that says "Statement," or "Receipt" in the subject to go straight to a folder marked Receipts. It doesn't distract her from important emails because she doesn't need to see most receipts.
- Bills that you have set up for autopay.

- Employee emails that don't pertain to you, like the company kickball team sign-up information, when you work remotely and aren't on the kickball team.

- Automatic responses or notifications.

- Industry news, professional development emails, or newsletters—I put all of these emails into a folder labeled *Friday* and choose to read them all on Fridays at once rather than getting distracted by them throughout the week.

- Emails that you are copied on are FYI and do not require you to do anything. I like this rule for my managers or people copied on everything. Instead, create a folder named *Copied,* and have any email that you are on the cc line go straight to that folder. Then, you can read them once per day, week, or whatever cadence makes sense to you.

- Personal emails that go to your work email address, such as your child's school emails.

TL;DR

Create rules or filters to automatically move emails to a folder or the trash so you see the higher-priority emails in your inbox.

Develop Email Templates

If you write the same or a similar email more than five times, stop rewriting and start using an email template, also known as a canned response or snippet, depending on the program you are using. Not only will this save you time, but it will also ensure that your answers are consistent. This method maintains uniformity in branding across your department if you have staff managing responses, too. You can always personalize, but remember that the less you write each time, the better.

Emails that can be templates include:

- Instructions to begin a project
- Client onboarding emails
- Responses to negative feedback or unhappy customers so you aren't emotionally charged when writing back
- Appointment scheduling information
- Instructions for the completion of a task
- Office hours, directions, and logistics
- Answers to frequently asked questions (FAQs)

Sample RaderCo templates:

- Media kit link
- Post-training materials and information
- Referral template for people to copy and paste when they want to introduce me
- Testimonial requests
- Client reference information
- Client onboarding
- Program questionnaires and feedback form

TL;DR

If you send similar emails frequently, use email templates. This saves time, ensures consistency, and maintains branding. Templates can be personalized but minimize repetitive writing. Examples include project instructions, responses to feedback, appointment info, FAQs, and client onboarding details.

MANAGERS

Create a Policy for Reply All

Stop the sprawl! Don't reply all!

When we survey companies to find out their email and messaging pains, the misuse of *reply all* is big. If everyone is complaining about it, who is doing it and why? Using it can flood inboxes with unnecessary emails and distract from high-priority emails. We may also include so many people that no one takes ownership, or fewer people read it because so many other people are on the thread. It can also just plain annoy people and create a negative work environment.

So why do people do it? A few reasons.

1) If the first person replies to everyone, others may feel they need to so that everyone knows they responded or have read it. They don't want to be the one person that doesn't respond. (Really, does everyone need to know that you congratulated Emily on her big promotion, or does only Emily need to know?).

2) They're afraid *not* to reply all because someone important may need to be on that email, and it's better to just include them, "just in case." They don't want to be blamed, so it's easier just to do it. ***Note: Justin Case is not your friend. He's a villain that will make you hoard things you don't need, create extra work, and stress you out. Ask yourself, what's the worst that could happen if I toss Justin Case to the curb? Bye-Bye Justin!*

3) To create transparency and ensure everyone knows their response (even when it doesn't apply to them).

4) It's their default setting, which can be changed.

Instead, as the sender, I recommend giving permission to respond *only to the sender*. If you write a group email and only need individual responses, at the bottom of your email, write "respond only to sender" or "no response necessary" if you don't need a response.

Discourage any acknowledgments like "got it" or "thanks" as a *reply all*.

Of course, there are times when the sender *does* need to be transparent, and it saves time and is informative for everyone to see your response. The bottom line is to be thoughtful. Think about whether the group needs to see your "thanks!" comments instead of your "I agree with Shannon on the move to Dayton" comments.

> *"Transparency is gold when it comes to psychological safety. Withholding information does lead to mistrust and anxiety. Teams can handle so much more than most share. Leaders sometimes hold back information which creates space for speculation, which is often far worse and more distracting than just knowing the real information." – Christina Rowe, Global Leadership and Learning Specialist*

Note about the use of bcc:

Bcc can be great for emails to which you only need individual responses. Even when recipients hit reply all, the message only goes to the sender. Any mass emails should be sent this way, especially if they are going external to the company so that email addresses aren't shared.

Don't use bcc if the transparency of who is on the email matters. For example, if I copy your manager, you should know I am copying your manager. As a recipient on bcc, I've made a mistake a couple of times by not realizing I was blind copied and responding, making the original sender look suspicious. Forwarding the email to the manager after you send it may be more appropriate. For example, A manager I was working with wanted their new clinical research associates to copy them on all the emails they sent to clinical investigators for the first month of employment. This was embarrassing to their direct reports (especially the experienced ones). The manager didn't need to see the reply of "confirmed" or the scheduling of meetings the investigator would reply with. Instead, I suggested that the associate bcc the manager so they didn't get the reply and they didn't feel like a "newbie" in their role.

I also like bcc when introducing someone. If I introduce Sara to Ryan, I hope Sara replies, "Thank you for the intro, Marcey! Moving you to bcc to spare your inbox." This way, I know that someone has taken over the conversation, and I can move on with my life without getting further back-and-forth emails.

Finally, don't use bcc if an email needs further explanation or discussion because others on the thread can't see all the individual responses.

TL;DR

Senders should explicitly state "respond only to sender" or "no response necessary" when appropriate. Discourage acknowledgments or one-word responses via reply all. Utilize bcc for mass emails that require individual responses, especially for external communications or confidential content, but avoid using bcc when transparency is important or further discussion is needed.

Implement Subject Lines and Naming Conventions

Effective email subject lines and naming conventions can make search and prioritization so much easier. Standardizing email naming conventions can ensure clarity and consistency across your team and company. A good subject line tells you the possible actions needed before opening the email. Let's transform your email habits from random to effective, one subject line at a time.

Writing "Action Requested" or AR and the due date or deadline in the subject line lets a person know they need to respond or do something by a specific time. When I put this in a subject line, it tells the person that if they have more urgent needs, they can get to my email later—saving them time—or it signals that mine is timely and needs to be prioritized.

Example: *Action Requested by September 2: Create Program Questionnaire and Flyer*

Writing "Not Urgent" in the subject line tells the recipient to skip opening the email until they have more time. I like to use this when I know someone has been on vacation or is overwhelmed with their workload.

Example: *Not Urgent: Additional photos for content repository*

One of my pet peeves is the subject line *Quick Question*. If it's quick, put the entire question in the subject line. If you can't put it in the subject line, then it's not a quick question. If it's just a one-liner, type it in the subject line followed by *End of Message* or *EOM*. One of my clients searched *"Quick Question,"* and 47 (!) emails came up. Not helpful for trying to find an archived email. This type of statement is best for a chat if it's internal.

Example: *Send Simpson report by Friday 5:00 p.m. EOM*

Naming conventions for consistency include using a client or project name at the beginning of the subject.

More naming conventions:

- FYI:
- Approval Needed:
- Update:
- Invitation:
- Follow-Up:
- Reminder:
- Announcement:
- Deadline:
- Due:
- Question:

TL;DR

Adopting clear and consistent naming conventions for subject lines can enhance your email management, making it easier to prioritize, sort, and respond effectively. This is one of the easiest ways to save *everyone* time.

Use Schedule Send

Scheduling emails to be sent at a later time offers several benefits:

- **Optimal Timing:** Ensures emails are received during business hours, increasing the likelihood of being read and responded to promptly.
- **Tech-Life Balance:** You can draft emails outside working hours without disturbing recipients' personal time.
- **Strategic Planning:** Write email follow-ups in advance so you don't forget.
- **Improved Productivity:** Helps manage and spread out your workload.
- **Error Reduction:** It provides a buffer period for reviewing and making necessary corrections before sending the email.

Delaying emails is also an easy way to reduce overwhelm, ensure your emails arrive at the most opportune time, and show your team you respect their time outside of work. I'm a big fan of delaying my emails and use it several times a day. With *Delay Send*, I can write the email as I'm thinking about it but postpone it. When and why would I want to do this?

- *For emails that require a decision like signing a contract or reviewing a proposal:* I want the recipient to get that email at a strategic time. For instance, I don't send these at the end of the day when the recipient is likely tired and may resort to a status quo or fear-based decision (aka answering "no"). I also don't recommend sending important emails on Friday afternoons.

- *For emails in the evenings or on the weekends when I might be working but don't want to steal someone else's evening or receive a response:* Note that if you are a manager or in a hierarchical position, many of your staff members will feel compelled to check their email if they know that you are working off-hours. You can tell them 100 times that you don't expect a response, but they'll probably check "just in case." Many will feel like they should go ahead and respond to you or at least check and then schedule *their* email to be delivered the next day. Just be courteous, take away the anticipatory stress, and schedule them!

Note: Some people prefer or must work at night and on weekends. You can consider whatever their "off-hours" might be instead. If you are dealing with people overseas and their 10:00 a.m. is your 8:00 p.m., it may not matter. The point is to consider who is receiving the email and their own time zone. There may not be a perfect time to send, but there can definitely be an *imperfect* time to send.

- *For people on vacation or traveling:* It's thoughtful to schedule these for a couple of days after they return. It may prevent them from getting lost in their inbox and also give them time to catch up on the other emails sent by people who don't practice this same etiquette.

- *For follow-up emails I don't want to forget to send:* I can schedule them days, weeks, or even months in advance. For example, If I have a question for my accountant during tax season, but it isn't urgent and has nothing to do with my taxes, I write the email and schedule it to be sent the first week of May.

- *To stop an email thread from going back and forth like a conversation:* If I've just received an email, I will even delay sending my response for ten minutes so they don't expect an immediate response in the future or a further conversation back-and-forth right then.

At the very least, avoid the Friday Dump. Receiving an email on Friday afternoon with a deliverable for Monday or anything that will make you shut down your computer and stress about it over the weekend is considered a "dump." Consider whether you would *call a person* and ask them to do something at the same time you are emailing. For example, would you call someone on Friday at 5:00 p.m. or Saturday at 10:00 a.m. and request they create a new presentation for you or ask for those numbers to finish your report? Probably not, but somehow, emailing the request seems culturally acceptable. Saving that email until the new workweek is more appropriate, and it lets people enjoy their weekends. If you want to work, that's fine, but you shouldn't expect others to work unless their job requires them to work on weekends. Schedule it to send on Monday. Don't be known as The Dumper.

> *"We learned that your inbox isn't just a hamster wheel where you're in there running and running. We need to think of it as the place where we talk to clients, and a space that needs boundaries. It was a helpful perspective shift that can stop your inbox from automatically triggering overwhelm." – Sophie Howell, Chief Operating Officer, Cook Wealth*

TL;DR

Scheduling emails for later enhances productivity and respect for recipients' time. It ensures optimal response timing, allows drafting during off-hours without disturbance, and facilitates strategic follow-ups. This practice reduces errors by providing review time and helps manage workload. It's ideal for decision-making emails, respecting personal time, considering time zones, and avoiding vacation inbox overload.

C+/BUSINESS OWNER

Designate No Email or Chat Times

Hold on to your coffee, and keep an open mind. Have you considered prohibiting or, at the very least, highly discouraging emails on certain days or specific times? Some companies have *No Email Fridays.* It's a movement where no email can be sent internally on Friday or, at a minimum, after noon on Friday. This may be challenging for many companies, especially if you're global, but it can be done! It keeps people from getting the Friday Dump and lets your team close out their tasks and go into the weekend feeling accomplished. Vynamic, a science consulting firm, encourages employees to refrain from sending emails in the evenings, on weekends, or Vynamic-observed holidays. They believe their progressive email policy supports work-life balance and promotes thoughtful communication.

If you default to thinking that a phone call takes longer than an email, consider how some long threads could have been completed over the phone in one minute or less. Make a rule for yourself and start with your team. Try calling or physically speaking to a team member on Fridays. Then, stretch this out to your department and later to the rest of your company. Who knows, you may even get your weekend back!

More companies with Email-Free Times

Deloitte - Some teams implement "quiet hours" when they don't allow emails or instant messages.

Volkswagen - Stops email servers after work hours to prevent after-hours communication.

Atlassian - Implements "Focus Fridays," where meetings and internal communication are minimized.

RaderCo isn't the typical 9-to-5 set-up. Sometimes, I work on Saturdays to spread out my work during the week or because I want to run errands or do "Saturday Stuff" on a weekday. I also like the quiet of working a little on Saturday. I may *process* email on a Friday or Saturday, but I always *schedule it* to go out on Monday or Tuesday. The fewer emails people have to read on the weekend, the better.

Even Slack, the world's second most popular instant messaging platform, doesn't keep Slack open all day. They get in and out and are discouraged from reacting to it. Their company culture encourages employees to work hard, go home, and *not* check their Slack after hours. Why did Slack adopt this policy? Among other statistics, they cite a survey of over 10,000 desk workers, which found that the most productive people were 1.7 times more likely to schedule time to process email rather than keep it open all day.[30]

Could you implement Focus Fridays, where no internal emails are sent? What about not emailing after a specific time in the evening or on weekends? Depending on the type of company, it may not be possible, but could you encourage people to shut down their instant messaging every day and not turn it on until one hour after they arrive, so they can get to their top tasks first and not get sucked into the ping and buzz vortex?

TL;DR

"No Email Fridays," focus hours, or quiet hours reduce distractions, improve task completion, and foster better communication.

> *"It used to be the expectation that if a client emailed us after hours, we should respond. After hearing Marcey's presentation on communication, our former CEO said he would no longer check or process email*

---

[30] "The Surprising Connection Between After-Hours Work and Decreased Productivity," Slack, December 5, 2023 (https://slack.com/blog/news/the-surprising-connection-between-after-hours-work-and-decreased-productivity)

after 5:30 p.m., and he didn't expect that we would either. It was a major shift." – Jason Deshayes, Chief Executive Officer, Cook Wealth

Develop a Communications Matrix

Implementing a communications matrix helps streamline communication and increase overall organizational efficiency. By defining clear channels for different types of communication or roles of recipients, you can ensure the right people are getting the right messages through the right channels and at the right times.

Problems:

- **Redundant Messages:** Employees often send repetitive emails or chat messages and spend approximately *2.5 hours daily* trying to find information.[31]

- **Overload:** An overwhelming number of messages can cause critical communications to get lost in the noise.

- **Delayed Responses:** A message sent through the wrong channel (e.g., a chat message when it would have been better sent through email) causes a delay.

- **Silos:** Sending a message via one channel that may not be accessible to someone else who needs it, slowing down decision-making and task completion.

---

[31] Leslie Hand and Anne Paris, "IDC Survey Spotlight: Workforce Transformation Challenges," IDC, June 2023 (https://www.idc.com/getdoc.jsp?containerId=US49080722)

- **Getting lost:** Sending a task in a chat may result in it getting lost because as the chatting goes on, the critical information gets pushed so far up in the thread they may have forgotten about it.

Implement a Communications Matrix that specifies the channels, protocols, and guidelines for various types of communication. Pilot it for one team and then have the broader company adopt it. Revisit it regularly to ensure it's working appropriately.

> One client in the aerospace and defense contracting industry tripled in size. The CEO continued to be copied on many emails, even though there were roles that were better suited to receive them. When Microsoft Teams was implemented, there was no training on when to use it vs email. It was overwhelming and confusing. Implementing a communications matrix ensured that the CEO was only copied on critical emails, such as when an opportunity over $1 million was at stake or potential litigation. Also important, they were specific about when the CEO shouldn't be copied, like customer order status, building and facilities concerns, or employee recognitions, because he could get the information in other ways, such as from a monthly report.

Matrix Column Considerations: If having this many columns is too much, start with a few and add on later.

Channels

- **Email:** For formal or detailed communication.
- **Chat Tools (e.g., Slack, Teams):** For quick questions and informal conversations.
- **Project Management Tools (e.g., Click-Up, Asana, Trello):** For task tracking and project updates.
- **Video Conferencing (e.g., Zoom, Teams):** For meetings (if asynchronous can't be used) and virtual face-to-face interactions.
- **Document Sharing (e.g., Google Drive, SharePoint):** For collaborative work and document management.

Usage

- **Urgent vs. Non-Urgent:** Clearly define what constitutes urgent communication and which channels should be used.
- **Information Type:** Announcements, feedback, routine updates.
- **Response Time:** Time expected for response.
- **Format:** Subject line naming conventions, hashtags.

Who and When

- **Receiver:** Who should be included and how in the To or cc.
- **Frequency:** How often certain communications should occur (e.g., weekly updates, daily check-ins).

Results:

Enhanced Clarity: Clear guidelines on where and how to communicate reduce confusion.

Improved Efficiency: Streamlined communication channels minimize redundant messages.

Increased Productivity: Employees spend less time managing communication and more time on their core tasks.

Better Collaboration: Centralized information and clear protocols foster teamwork and information sharing.

TL;DR

Implementing a communications matrix can help companies reduce the volume of unnecessary emails and chat messages, decrease confusion, and minimize redundant messages. This leads to a more efficient and focused work environment with better collaboration (and fewer lost tasks!).

Get your copy of a sample Communications Matrix by going to reclaimyourworkday.com.

References

Radica Boshnjakoska, "How Many Emails Are Sent per Day in 2024?," Review 42, February 13, 2024 (https://review42.com/resources/how-many-emails-are-sent-per-day/)

Jayson DeMers, "Email Productivity Benchmark Report (May 2023)," Email Analytics (https://emailanalytics.com/email-productivity-benchmark-report/)

Hazel Emnace, "17 Business Email Statistics and Trends to Watch in 2024," Fit Small Business, November 23, 2023 (https://fitsmallbusiness.com/business-email-statistics-and-trends/)

Judith Guertin and Barbara Hemphill, *Taming the Digital Tiger: A Step-by-Step Guide to Tame Your Gmail Account in No Time Flat,* Write Way Publishing Company, February 10, 2021 (https://www.abebooks.com/9781946425829/Taming-Digital-Tiger-Step-by-Step-Guide-1946425826/plp)

Leslie Hand and Anne Paris, "IDC Survey Spotlight: Workforce Transformation Challenges," IDC, June 2023 (https://www.idc.com/getdoc.jsp?containerId=US49080722)

Jory MacKay, "Communication Overload: Our Research Shows Most Workers Can't Go 6 Minutes Without Checking Email or IM," RescueTime, July 11, 2018 (https://blog.rescuetime.com/communication-multitasking-switches/)

"Email Statistics Report 2021-2025" Radicati Group, Inc., February 2021 (https://www.radicati.com/

wp/wp-content/uploads/2020/12/Email-Statistics-Report-2021-2025-Executive-Summary.pdf)

"Stress in America 2020," American Psychological Association, October 1, 2020 (https://www.apa.org/news/press/releases/stress/2020/report-october)

"The Surprising Connection Between After-Hours Work and Decreased Productivity," Slack, December 5, 2023 (https://slack.com/blog/news/the-surprising-connection-between-after-hours-work-and-decreased-productivity)

CHAPTER 3

MEETINGS

Unproductive meetings are a significant drain on resources and productivity. A staggering 71% of meetings are deemed unproductive, resulting in an annual loss of $37 billion for U.S. companies. Employees spend an average of 31 hours per month in these unproductive gatherings. Furthermore, 92% of employees admit to multitasking during meetings, with 69% checking emails and 49% engaging in unrelated activities. Unsurprisingly, 67% of executives consider most meetings a failure. This inefficiency not only wastes time but also hampers overall productivity and morale.[32]

When was the last time you asked for feedback on a meeting? On an average scale of 1-10, how productive are your meetings? How many meetings in the past week did you leave feeling energized and excited and that you got something done?

---

[32] Barry Elad, "29+ Amazing Meeting Statistics 2023: Virtual vs. In-Person Meeting, Zoom, and Productivity," Enterprise Apps Today, October 4, 2023 (https://www.enterpriseappstoday.com/stats/meeting-statistics.html)

Unproductive meetings have a huge business cost.

Besides metrics like productivity and time, these unproductive meetings also have a business cost—in terms of dollars—attached to them. Assuming an average employee makes $60,000 per year and a company has 100 employees, the cost of meetings rises to $2,250,000, while the price of unproductive meetings per year is $751,500.[33]

You can use Otter.AI's cost calculator to estimate the cost of unproductive meetings in your business (https://otter.ai/meeting-cost-calculator).

There's also the problem of too many meetings getting in the way of focused work. Many of my corporate clients work for companies where they have back-to-back meetings, without any break, for six hours at a time, several days per week. They get tasks they are supposed to complete during their meetings, yet there is no space in their calendars to complete them. They are often hired for their strategy or subject matter expertise, but they get no time to develop either one.

Since 2013, RaderCo has been surveying its clients on their productivity behaviors, and over half of respondents admit to multitasking during meetings. If you can check your email while in a meeting, you don't need to be in that meeting! I imagine it's like the phenomenon of illusory superiority, where 93% of

---

[33] Chang Chen, "Shocking Meeting Statistics in 2021 That Will Take You By Surprise," Otter.AI, December 24, 2020 (https://otter.ai/blog/meeting-statistics)

Americans believe they are above-average drivers.[34] I bet 93% of people in meetings think others can't tell when they are also checking their messages or otherwise distracted. Improving how you do meetings is one of the most significant changes you can make on the journey to reclaiming your workday.

Meetings are where productivity goes to die—unless you take control. Imagine a world where meetings are efficient, engaging, and purposeful. No more aimless discussions or endless scheduling conflicts. This chapter will revolutionize how you view and conduct meetings. Implementing strategies that declutter your agenda and streamline your focus will transform meetings from time sinks to powerful productivity tools. Get ready to learn the secrets of running meetings that leave you and your team energized, aligned, and ready to tackle what truly matters.

TL;DR

Unproductive meetings cost U.S. companies $37 billion annually. Seventy-one percent of meetings are ineffective due to multitasking (92%), lack of clear agendas (40%), and poor communication. Employees spend 31 hours monthly in such meetings, and 67% of executives find them unproductive. Key solutions include implementing "no devices" policies, distributing clear agendas, providing platform training, regularly reviewing meeting logistics, setting clear objectives,

---

[34] Ola Svenson, "Are We All Less Risky and More Skillful Than Our Fellow Drivers?," Acta Psychologica, 1981 (https://web.archive.org/web/20120722210701/http://heatherlench.com/wp-content/uploads/2008/07/svenson.pdf)

managing time effectively, limiting attendees, and ensuring accountability for action items.

Problems:

- **Multitasking and Distractions**: Ninety-two percent of employees multitask during meetings by checking emails (69%) and performing unrelated tasks (49%).[35]

- **Lack of Preparation**: Nearly 40% of workplace meetings lack a clear agenda, leading to aimless discussions and unproductive outcomes.[36] People often skip pre-work, expecting it will be discussed during the meeting anyway. Over-ambitious agendas also dilute focus.

- **Technical Issues in Virtual Meetings**: Connectivity issues and having to learn new platforms cause inefficiency and frustration.[37]

- **Meeting Overload**: Employees spend a significant portion of their workday in meetings. There are too many meetings, too often, with too many people.

---

[35] Barry Elad, "29+ Amazing Meeting Statistics 2023: Virtual vs. In-Person Meeting, Zoom, and Productivity," Enterprise Apps Today, October 4, 2023 (https://www.enterpriseappstoday.com/stats/meeting-statistics.html)

[36] "Meeting Statistics: Effectiveness, Virtual Conferencing, and More in 2024," Teamstage (https://teamstage.io/21-monumental-meeting-statistics/)

[37] Barry Elad, "29+ Amazing Meeting Statistics 2023: Virtual vs. In-Person Meeting, Zoom, and Productivity," Enterprise Apps Today, October 4, 2023 (https://www.enterpriseappstoday.com/stats/meeting-statistics.html)

Recurring meetings aren't regularly evaluated for necessity.[38]

- **Unproductive Meeting Culture**: Sixty-seven percent of meetings are considered unproductive by executives, often due to poor communication, lack of follow-up, and insufficient time management.[39]

- **Engagement Issues**: Thirty-seven percent of meetings start late, leading to a loss of focus and productivity. Many employees feel their ideas aren't appreciated, causing disengagement.[40]

- **Inviting too many people:** Video meetings often include too many participants, creating bottlenecks. *Not every decision needs consensus.*

- **No Accountability for Action Items:** Action items often need to be clarified and have no designated follow-up, leading to confusion and inaction.

Solutions:

- **No Devices:** Implement a "no device" policy. For in-person meetings, phones and laptops are put away; only a primary notetaker or presenter can use their

---

[38] Eric Moore, "31 Need-To-Know Meeting Statistics (2023 Update): Virtual, Zoom, In-Person, Productivity," Overheard on Conference Calls, March 2, 2023 (https://overheardonconferencecalls.com/business/meeting-statistics/)

[39] "Meeting Statistics: Effectiveness, Virtual Conferencing, and More in 2024," Teamstage (https://teamstage.io/21-monumental-meeting-statistics/)

[40] "Meeting Statistics: Effectiveness, Virtual Conferencing, and More in 2024," Teamstage (https://teamstage.io/21-monumental-meeting-statistics/)

computer. For virtual meetings, participants should completely shut out email and chat tools.

> *Note: If you rely on your laptop to take notes and are "allergic" to my no-devices policy, know that taking notes on a computer is less effective. You retain less information because you are writing word for word when typing. When writing by hand, you tend to write only the main points.*

- **Distribute Clear Agendas:** Emphasize pre-work. Don't provide status updates for a few unprepared individuals. Prioritize items to keep meetings focused.

- **Provide Training on the Platform:** Provide brief training for new updates and establish a technical support system to handle connectivity issues.

- **Evaluate Meeting Logistics:** Regularly review the frequency, length, and attendees of recurring meetings. Short meetings should be 15-25 minutes long, and longer meetings 45-50 minutes long.

- **Set Clear Objectives:** Ensure follow-ups on tasks and make people accountable for their action items.

- **Time Management:** Start and end meetings on time. Keep discussions relevant to maintain engagement.

- **Limit Attendees** Invite only essential participants. Each person should have a specific role or purpose.

- **Accountability for Action Items:** Clearly define action items and assign responsibilities before the meeting ends. Use tools to track progress and follow up regularly.

Levels

Action steps for Individuals:
- Avoid Autopilot Attendance
- Incorporate Video Screen Capture
- Improve Your Virtual Set-Up

Action steps for Managers:
- Implement Office Hours
- Structure One-to-Ones or 1:1s

Action Steps for C+/Business Owners:
- Create Meeting Foundations
- Enlist Scheduling Options
- Implement Meeting-Free Days or Weeks

INDIVIDUAL

Avoid Autopilot Attendance

How many meetings are you attending without considering whether you really need to be there? If you didn't receive an agenda and doubt why you are there, ask! You may assume you must be there when the inviter isn't sure and invited you... Justin Case (and we all know what a time-waster he can be). You lose an hour of your time and may even create a bottleneck because there are too many opinions and yours wasn't even really needed (sorry).

If *you* are inviting someone else to a meeting, instead of just sending an invite, ask them, based on the content of the meeting, if they could contribute something. If not, don't steal their hour. No one has time for nice-to-have people at their meetings.

Invite only those people whose input is essential to the topic. Be considerate of duplication of efforts and inviting more than one person from a department who can make the same decision or contribution. If you wouldn't need their input on a specific question during a round-robin, is it necessary for them to attend the meeting? Yes, we all think our input is invaluable, and we can't imagine anyone would have such a fantastic idea as ours, but let's set down our cognitive dissonance and recognize that *we aren't needed all the time for everything*, even meetings.

My rule is if I'm optional, I'm not needed. Optional doesn't mean anything. Get out of the habit of ever asking someone to attend optionally. When attendees don't have to be mentally present, it can lead to ineffective discussions and decisions. They are most likely multitasking, which is evident to everyone and makes others feel disengaged.

Multitasking can have worse consequences, too. While I was presenting virtually to a team, a woman came off of mute and said, "I feel like I'm getting yelled at." and then dropped off the call. It was in the first ten minutes of the training, and I didn't know what happened. I felt terrible and distracted because I didn't know what I had said to make her feel that way, and I'm sure people on the call were wondering what was happening. It certainly set a tone. After the call, I spoke to the Director who hired me and asked her to please check with the attendee. After a week of losing sleep at night because I felt so awful and wanted to know how I may have offended her (I really do care!), the Director got back to me. The attendee had no idea they were unmuted and had been multitasking. In Zoom, when you press the spacebar, it unmutes you, and she had been talking to a coworker. Her statement had nothing to do with the presentation (which she was disappointed that she had to leave). In this case, this meeting and email multitasking habit that we all have resulted in a distracted presentation, lost sleep, editing of the video and transcript, her feeling embarrassed, and a week of angst for me!

A Slack survey of over 10,000 desk workers found that more than two hours of meetings in a day cut into focused work time.[41] While a day with only two hours of meetings may feel luxurious to some, you could still consider having a weekly meeting budget. Maybe you can allot 20 hours per week. Anything over that 20 hours means you either have to remove something from your calendar, shorten a meeting (if you are the host), or decline the new invitation.

To be the owner of your calendar, look at it one month out and determine which meetings are genuinely required. Look first at your recurring meetings. If you are the person running them, see if they can be done less frequently or if they can be done in

---

[41] "The Surprising Connection Between After-Hours Work and Decreased Productivity," Slack, December 5, 2023 (https://slack.com/blog/news/the-surprising-connection-between-after-hours-work-and-decreased-productivity)

a shorter time frame. People tend to keep going with the same frequency and time of meetings, even when they don't need to. Can a meeting be done once a week for 15 minutes instead of 30? Can it be changed to every two weeks instead of weekly as the project progresses?

Own your time! Reclaim your workday!

TL;DR

Question your meeting invites. If there's no agenda and you doubt your necessity, ask! Unnecessary invites waste time and create bottlenecks. If inviting others, ensure they can contribute meaningfully. "Optional" attendees aren't needed. Only essential participants should attend to avoid ineffective discussions and multitasking. Be considerate of duplication of efforts and invite only those truly required.

Incorporate Video Screen Capture

I often hear that a meeting "could have been just an email," "wasn't required," "could have been way shorter," "had no clear objectives," and "was hard to follow because we had no context for the meeting." Video screen-capture software like Loom can help shorten or replace meetings or prepare team members for upcoming meetings.

Screen-capture software allows users to record their computer screen's activity and explanation, capturing images or videos of what's displayed. You don't have to appear on camera yourself, which is useful when you aren't "camera ready."

Features typically include:

1. Screenshot: Capture a still image of the entire screen or a specific area.

2. Screen Recording: Record video of on-screen actions, including mouse movements and clicks (very helpful when showing how to navigate something).

3. Annotations: Add notes, arrows, or highlights to capture your ideas.

4. Editing: Trim or remove parts you don't want in the final version.

5. Sharing: Easily share captured content via email, cloud storage, or social media.

6. Speed: Watch at a slower speed or make it go faster.

7. Transcription: Read along with the video.

8. Watcher annotations: The person watching can make comments or ask questions at points throughout the video.

At RaderCo, we use screen-capture software, sometimes multiple times a day, instead of meeting. We prefer Loom because of its ease of use and many features, but there are others you can test.

For our meetings, if there is something that we need to go over, let's say, a concept or a new brand guide, I will make a five-minute or less video ahead of time. I will send it to my team so they have that context before the meeting. They can review it, know what we will discuss, and bring their ideas.

This solves the biggest unproductive meetings problem, i.e., lack of participant preparation.[42]

> A coaching client at a biotech company reviewed the team's yearly goals during a meeting. When I told the client about using video software to shorten meetings, she said she could have given their team these goals beforehand. The team would have had time to think about it before coming in, and the meeting could have been more impactful. As it was, they had to have another meeting about the information she had shared. Video software could have eliminated that second meeting.

For instance, if you're an accountant, you could use this trick to train your clients on their tax portal. You can share your screen and do a screen capture, talking through the tool. That could be even more helpful than a meeting because they have that recording and can use it whenever they need to access the portal.

Why use screen capture instead of just opening up Teams or Zoom to do a video? With something like Loom, it's an extension in the browser, so it's really fast to record. It's also available immediately without waiting to download and sync to a folder. It's much quicker to edit since most video software has limited capabilities after something is recorded

---

[42] Chang Chen, "Shocking Meeting Statistics in 2021 That Will Take You By Surprise," Otter.AI, December 24, 2020 (https://otter.ai/blog/meeting-statistics)

(if they have the capabilities built in at all). Often, with regular video conferencing recordings, you have to upload them to a different program to edit. If you choose to download, files are also smaller with Loom, making storing easier.

More examples of video screen capture uses:

Processing Marcey's email: I go through my emails and explain how I want them processed while away. This way, any member of my team can complete this task.

Outlook Tips: I created a series of Outlook Quick Tips videos for a client that they downloaded and hosted on their Microsoft Teams site.

Sample conference application: I walked through how to complete a conference application and find all the submission materials so any team member could do it.

Audible book distribution: Steps to deliver Audible books to my clients.

How to complete the Team Specialist coaching sheet: Instead of training each new Team Specialist, I only have to send them this video.

How to get to our Office: My client Jim has an office space that is confusing to find. He created a Loom on his phone from the street to the parking garage to the office. Clients have loved it, and the visual context is more useful than an email someone's trying to read to "imagine" where they are going.

Website edits: I can scroll through my website and easily discuss what I want changed.

Technical support: When I experience a glitch, I capture my movements on screen to share with technical support so they can better understand my problem.

Proposal walk-through: I'm often on a call with one to two people, but others are involved in deciding to hire us. So, I create a five-minute video walking through the proposal. This way, the initial person doesn't have to remember everything I said, and those people don't have to meet or can have a shorter meeting to make their decision.

TL;DR

Replace or shorten meetings using video screen-capture software like Loom. Record your screen to create tutorials, explain concepts, or provide context before meetings. This approach improves preparation, saves time, and enhances clarity. Examples include technical support issues, client portal tips, and proposal walk-throughs. It's fast and easy to edit, and files are smaller for easier storage and sharing. Incorporate screen-capture videos to enhance productivity and communication and save yourself from a meeting (or two!)

Improve Your Virtual Set-Up

No longer does anyone have an excuse not to have some kind of virtual set-up that looks professional. Even if you aren't a remote worker, you may still have virtual meetings with your clients, and people are now more used to video than the phone. I always give Speaker Connection Calls, Coaching Discovery

Calls, and Virtual Coffees the choice to meet via Zoom or Phone. The preference is about 60/40 video to the phone.

Some key items to consider:

Environment: Your space should be quiet with minimal distractions and noise. If the lawnmower is running at home or you have a loud talker for a deskmate, keep your video on mute until it's your turn to speak.

Background: Have an uncluttered, professional background. If you have a lot of stuff behind you, people will look at it and not focus on you. If you use a virtual background, make sure it isn't distracting. You don't want to look like you're in a jungle or a child at a circus. I'm not a big fan of virtual backgrounds unless they are so good that people compliment you on your 'office,' and you don't "lose" your hair, arm, or anything else if you move even a few inches. Before I built my studio, my trick was a simple roll of paper hanging from the ceiling that I rolled down behind me while on video.

I also recommend using a virtual background or the blur feature if people walk behind you, whether at home, in the office, or at a coffee shop. Seeing other people in the background distracts people on video, and we sometimes wonder, "Does their husband know they are on a call?" "What is that person reaching for?" It's less distracting in person because we can view the full context of the room or environment.

Webcams: Most newer computers have great webcams, but I suggest buying an external one that you can mount, which makes the angle nicer for people to see you and is flattering.

Note: If you are looking at a different monitor to see the person you're talking to and not directly at the camera, let them know you are looking at them. Before every presentation, I tell people, "If I'm looking here, I'm looking at the chat. If I'm looking here, I'm looking at the camera, and here I'm looking at your faces." I've had many compliments and "thank yous" for letting them know where my eyes are (and that I'm not looking at my email or someone else in the room!).

Microphone and Headset: A good quality microphone that makes you sound clear can make a world of difference. A headset can keep the extraneous noise in your house or office at a minimum or silenced. If you are working from home and people know that there are other people at home with you, it can cause anxiety that they will hear your conversation. Even if it's not confidential, it still feels awkward. Wear headphones.

Stable Internet Connection: This is essential for smooth video calls and reducing frustration. Know how to use your phone's hotspot as a backup if your internet goes out. If possible, hardwire your computer. I have super fast Google Fiber WiFi, but I'm still always hard-wired when presenting and on coaching calls.

Lighting: If possible, face a window and use a ring light or desk lamp to eliminate shadows.

Ergonomics: An adjustable desk that allows you to sit or stand will give you options and keep you from feeling like a potted plant or toy soldier all day, stiff from not moving because you're in too many meetings. If you're presenting, try to stand. Being on your feet tends to make you more engaged, and it's more natural. You want the camera positioned so attendees aren't looking up your nose or are blocked from seeing half your forehead.

Software Updates: Check regularly that you have the latest version installed of whatever software you're using.

Look Like You Tried: You may have a casual company culture, but we've gotten a little too casual, in my opinion. At the least, dress up from the chest up and wear something you'd wear in the office or with a client. Yes, I once made the mistake of wearing a shirt and jacket on top and running shorts on the bottom (it was 101 degrees in July) and stepped away from the computer to grab something. The client and I laughed about it, but I didn't make that mistake again, and now I turn off my camera or wear something that's not running shorts! I also keep an "office jacket or scarf" beside my desk that I throw on for meetings and always put on some kind of jewelry.

TL;DR

A professional virtual set-up starts with a quiet, distraction-free environment and a clean background. Use a high-quality, adjustable webcam and inform participants where you're looking. Invest in a good microphone and headset to ensure clear communication. Maintain a stable internet connection, using a hotspot as backup and a hardwired connection when possible. Proper lighting, such as facing a window or using a ring light, is essential. Use an adjustable desk to switch between sitting and standing. Regularly update your meeting software and dress professionally, at least from the chest up, to convey the right impression.

MANAGER

Implement Office Hours

I discussed Office Hours in Chapter 1 to minimize distractions and ensure managers have time to do the most important strategic work. This same tactic can cut down on unnecessary meetings, too. Many leaders feel they have to be Siri or Alexa, always available with an answer for their teams. Being reactive like this can set a bad example, cause anticipatory stress for you because you're always waiting for the next ping, promote errors, and disempower your team from finding the answer themselves. Unless your job is just to answer questions, you probably have other "zone of genius" work you must do. Setting up office hours can give you focus time and less anxiety about when you will be available for your team.

Example for in the office:

Keep your door open, put up a sign, or otherwise make it known that daily from x time to x time (e.g., 4:00-5:15 p.m.), anyone can stop by with any questions or whatever they want to share. This is especially useful for something often put in an email or chat that becomes a back-and-forth conversation. It's much more efficient to use our mouths and quickly discuss it and knock it out. Because you are visible, people can see when others are in the room and can wait or queue up.

Example for remote employees:

Set up your virtual meeting using the same link every time, ideally at the same time every day or at the cadence you want to offer it. Team members can work independently in the "waiting room" while you let people in one by one to answer questions or share information. Because they know someone may be waiting, they (and you) will be more succinct and get to the point. When you're done, they exit, and you let the next person in. I've participated in coaching calls this way, and it works out great!

If you aren't a manager but have another role where people often ask questions, you can also set these up. Weekly or daily HR, Benefits, and IT office hours could eliminate long email chains. You could also test this with customers. Depending on your business, you could offer a weekly Ask Us Anything, and customers could join and learn about the software, product, or anything else they may need help with.

TL;DR

Office hours can improve productivity, reduce stress, and replace unnecessary meetings. Instead of always being available, leaders can set specific times for questions, fostering focused work for them and empowering teams. In the office, designate daily open-door periods for quick discussions. For remote teams, use a consistent virtual meeting link with a waiting room for efficient interactions. This approach also benefits roles like HR, IT, or customer support, streamlining communication and enhancing efficiency.

Structure One-to-Ones or 1:1s

One-to-one or 1:1 meetings are frequently discussed in coaching sessions at RaderCo. Employees often feel like they are a waste of time and leaders aren't always sure how to lead them. They become a manager and "poof" are expected to know what to ask, what feedback to give, and how to handle one-to-one meetings.

We heard this complaint so many times we created a program that I had already been using personally since 2012, the Powered Path Program™. It's a one-hour online microlearning productivity course to aid with reflection, planning, and prioritizing. It comes with a digital playbook. More details are in the next chapter, so I'll focus here on how it can work for 1:1s. Whether you use this tool or not, come up with a template to hit these critical components.

> *"Let your direct report drive the agenda for your one-to-one meeting. Before running through your agenda items, give them time to discuss what's on their mind. This conveys that you respect them and are interested in what is important to them." – Wendy Gates Corbett, RaderCo Belonging and Culture Specialist*

Lack of Clear Agenda: Meetings without a specific agenda often waste time and lack focus. For 1:1s, the team member should be driving their meeting and come with the items they want to discuss. Create templates for your team so they can check in regularly on their Daily, Weekly, Monthly, Quarterly, and Annual priorities and ensure they align with what you think they should be. Also, give them space to keep track of their Big Wins, Lessons Earned (because we *earn* our battle scars), Smartest Decisions, and more. Having templates for these check-ins ensures that you're getting the same information from everyone, and come review time, it's not as daunting of a task for them or you to try and remember what they did six months ago.

It also helps people who don't feel comfortable sharing their accomplishments. Since it's a regular question on the template, they are expected to answer it. The same goes for sharing their mistakes. If they aren't making mistakes, they probably aren't growing much or being challenged! Keep a shared document with the agenda, or use a standard template so each of you can add to it as you think of things you want to discuss.

Over-Scheduling: Too many meetings can lead to calendar clutter, and 1:1s often get deprioritized and canceled. Be careful about scheduling too many in one day since the person at the end of the day may get the tired leader who is less engaged. On another note, sometimes leaders require weekly meetings when that person only needs every other week. Some schedule 30 minutes weekly, but 45 minutes every other week would be optimal and less disruptive. If someone is new, they may prefer to meet every week. Regularly check in with the cadence and amount of time. It doesn't have to be cookie-cutter, where every team member has to be the same. Ask them what they need and discuss what seems optimal.

> *"The leaders I consult with consistently tell me they are astounded at the impact one simple behavior has on the quality of their one-to-ones with their direct reports. The behavior: closing their laptop at the beginning of a meeting. This one action conveys to the employee: you are more important than anything*

on my computer. In meetings, give your employees (and colleagues) your undistracted attention." – Wendy Gates Corbett, RaderCo Belonging and Culture Specialist

Lack of Follow-Up: Action items may be forgotten or neglected without proper follow-up. Recording your discussions can help you remember their performance during review time, monitor their workload and priorities, and understand what they desire from their job or role. These action items should be reviewed before each 1:1.

Create a Safe Space: Foster an environment where employees feel comfortable sharing concerns and ideas. Promote Powered Path questions like "what worked well?" and "what didn't work well?" so they get used to sharing without fearing repercussions. Ask them regularly about bottlenecks and create a culture of embracing them,[43] because if we don't identify and share them, they'll continue to wreak havoc on our efficiency. This safe space also includes your undivided attention. Shut down your email and chat tool, and put your phone away.

> *"Psychological safety is really the solid foundation that everything else builds from with any sustainability. To be innovative, productive, or deeply engaged you need psychological safety. When people feel seen, heard, valued, and safe they can focus on their work and the best solutions possible. If there isn't psychological safety, then we're constantly distracted or anxious trying to evaluate what the right move is*

---

[43] Marcey Rader, "Embrace the Bottlenecks," RaderCo (https://www.helloraderco.com/bottlenecks/)

over the right thing for the organization or the right
solution to a problem." – Christina Rowe, Global
Leadership and Learning Specialist

Discuss Career Development: Regularly explore long-term goals and aspirations and identify opportunities for growth and development. Not everyone knows the paths they can choose or what's available. Find out what they want long-term and set a plan to get them there.

Encourage Two-Way Feedback: Ask for feedback on your leadership and the effectiveness of the meetings. I managed 18 first-time Clinical Research Associates and had 45-minute meetings with them every other week. I also had a 15-minute check-in on the off-weeks. One employee felt empowered to tell me she didn't need that. She was more experienced than the others, and it was disruptive to her day. I appreciated her telling me that and asked the rest of the team if they wanted the 15-minute meetings. Most said yes, others asked for it for a specific period, like two more months, and two others said they didn't need them. It freed up time, but more importantly, it made me realize that one size doesn't fit all and to always ask for feedback on my meetings.

TL;DR

One-to-one meetings often feel unproductive. RaderCo's Powered Path Program™, a one-hour microlearning course, offers structure with clear agendas, ensures follow-up, and fosters open communication. It includes a playbook and makes one-to-ones more effective and meaningful through a consistent template and two-way feedback.

C+/BUSINESS OWNER

Create Meeting Foundations

Companies that decide on productive policies and practices for their meetings fare better than those that operate like the Wild West. Often, those policies get broken or aren't abided by...executive leadership. I cannot stress enough that *you* are also the Chief Meetings Officer, and if you run over your time, don't provide an agenda, or are multitasking, you are giving silent permission that others can do the same, that your time is more valuable and respected than theirs, and that can create a sense of friction and frustration for your employees.

> *"Our team does our best to avoid scheduling meetings during anyone's lunch hour in their time zone. We also refrain from scheduling meetings after 1:00 pm EST on Fridays." – Tanya Jones-Fosu, Senior Director of Category Leadership, KIND*

I've consulted and trained companies on meeting foundations, and I'm providing some below for you to consider for your own policies.

The Rule of Seven or the Two-Pizza Rule: The Rule of Seven states that for every person over seven in a meeting, decision-making decreases by 10%. It's not just too many cooks in the kitchen that spoil the broth. People do not pay attention if 15 or 20 people are in a meeting. Smaller groups are more effective for decision-making and participation. Remember, inclusion doesn't mean consensus. Not everyone has to be invited to a meeting. This also allows room for everyone to contribute, and you're more likely to stay on topic.

Jeff Bezos calls this the Two-Pizza rule. The idea is that there are too many people if you can't feed the group with two pizzas.[44] Remember, ten people in a room or virtual conference isn't a one-hour meeting; it's a ten-hour meeting. People who pay by the hour and invite contractors to meetings are often much more mindful of how many people they invite to the table because they can see how much it costs them in dollars.

Determine if it could be an email: Are you just giving status updates? A Project Management System could alleviate this, but so could a shared document that everyone has to update by a specific time and date each week/day, etc., and then assign a window of time for everyone to review it.

Start meetings on time: A whopping 37% of meetings start late, which can cause frustration and make people who do show up on time feel disrespected. They would have also liked to have had that extra two minutes to refill their coffee or use the restroom. Meeting facilitators should foster a culture of starting on time.[45]

---

[44] Stephanie, Mickelson, "How You Can Use Jeff Bezos' Two-Pizza Rule to Find Career and Financial Success," Yahoo Finance, April 24, 2024 (https://finance.yahoo.com/news/jeff-bezos-two-pizza-rule-130039391.html?guccounter=1&guce_referrer=aHR0cHM6Ly93d3cuZ29vZ2xlLmNvbS8&guce_referrer_sig=AQAAAGOvjQ8kHCA8e4M8Qus8CVeuRo3mMksBFfKtEA32jSxNw0iuvcxPbgBWQrQN01OuvMVRV6CM5mbwQzUP forA-ysy5TE666TLPCl4n67xyT8ue7cUdpBZYZUYuUCwB5g8 guJ-h4VdVyVjTVaEEwLuemp161DpQmAkcEJuiGvY42vx)

[45] "Techsmith's Async-First Study Eliminated Meetings and Saw +15% Increase in Employee Productivity," Techsmith, January 10, 2023 (https://www.techsmith.com/press/latest/async-first-experiment/)

Meetings should not end at the hour: 15, 25, 45, or 50-minute meetings should be the rule. There is nothing magical about ending on the hour. Instead, it makes people who have back-to-back meetings anxious about making it to their next meeting, contributes to the problem of meetings starting late, doesn't provide time to process the meeting and create tasks or take notes to follow up on, or even time to take a biology or water break! I know people who have almost peed their pants *in their own house* because of so many back-to-back meetings.

You can set the default in your calendar tool to end meetings early. I recommend that IT set this up as the default for all new computers. I have been asked about starting all meetings five or ten minutes *after* the hour instead. I don't recommend it. It's harder for our brains to process this, and it can cause even more anxiety about missing meetings.

And while we're on the subject of magical times, there's also nothing magical about a 15-minute notification reminder. Who needs 15 minutes? Instead, change it to five or zero if you always look at your calendar like me. Because once that notification goes off, if you were in deep work mode, you aren't anymore and can't get back to it before that meeting. Also, shortening the 15-minute reminder to five can actually prevent people from showing up late, so you can start all meetings on time. Most people don't need 15 minutes to prepare for a meeting. They are already in a meeting or may be focused on a task. If they are interrupted with 15 minutes to go, they aren't going to be able to get back to their same level of focus and have now lost ten minutes of time.

Require agendas and minutes or actions for every meeting:
No agenda needed? Then why are we having a meeting? Make
sure every meeting has an agenda by putting it in the calendar
invite or, my preference, a shared document so others can add
to it if needed. This should be done at *least* 24 to 48 hours
before the meeting so people know what they are expected to
contribute and if they are actually required to do so. Before
the meeting, the facilitator should prioritize what to discuss.
You can use an AI transcription summary or some kind of
transcript to send out after the meeting. Bold or highlight
the action items to clarify Who, What, and When. After
every meeting, I send the Zoom AI summary to attendees or
coaching clients. The transcription isn't perfect, but it's good
enough to remind people of what we discussed, and it does a
great job of capturing Action Items and Next Steps.

Schedule with at least 48 hours notice: Turning on your
computer to find out you have a new meeting on your calendar
since you clocked out yesterday can derail someone's entire
day. Avoid scheduling last-minute meetings unless they are
truly urgent.

Have meeting roles: People should take turns facilitating since
it's a valuable skill for everyone to develop. The Timer or Meeting
Maestro will keep everyone on track and prevent individuals
from dominating the conversation. Our client Horizon Farm
Credit uses the acronym ELMO—Enough, Let's Move On. If
you use the Zoom platform, you can use the embedded timer
app so everyone can see how much time they have to speak. It
keeps people on track, especially if they are unaware of their
talkative nature. In person? Use something like the Time Timer
and watch the red countdown timer go down.

Fun acronyms:

FOCUS – Fast, Organized, Clear, Useful, Short

"Let's FOCUS!" to keep things concise and on track.

PAUSE – Purposeful, Actionable, Useful, Short, Effective

"Time to PAUSE!" to ensure discussions are purposeful and efficient.

SNAP – Stay Necessary, Accurate, Prompt

"Let's SNAP to it!" to keep conversations necessary and prompt.

BOLT – Brief, On-point, Logical, Timely

"Let's BOLT this!" to ensure the meeting stays logical and timely.

TRIM – Targeted, Relevant, Important, Managed

"Let's TRIM the fat!" to keep the focus on what's essential and managed.

Whatever policies you choose to implement as your meeting foundations, revisit them regularly. Employees forget, and new employees join the company. One company invested considerable time and money into creating a meeting foundations policy and training but didn't prioritize revisiting it once or twice a year and relied on certain team members to share the message. Some of those team members forgot the foundations themselves or weren't aware that it was their responsibility, so the enthusiasm waned, and many got back into old, bad habits. Add an automatic reminder on the calendar to revisit at least yearly.

TL;DR

The Rule of Seven or the Two-Pizza Rule, states that meetings should have no more than seven participants to maintain efficiency and boost focus and participation. Use email or shared documents for status updates. Start meetings on time and schedule them for 15, 25, 45, or 50 minutes to prevent back-to-back stress. Always require an agenda and action items, and schedule meetings with at least 48 hours notice. Assign roles, rotate facilitators, and use timers to stay on track.

Enlist Scheduling Options

Many scheduling systems on the market allow people to see available blocks on their calendars and request an appointment. If you spend your time doing the email dance to schedule a simple appointment, start using a system. Check out software like Breely or Calendly, or others suitable for your business. You can create different lengths and locations of meetings and sync events with your Google or Outlook calendars so you never have to remember to post your availability. For people who think it's rude to provide a link, some people like me think it's disrespectful to expect me to go back and forth with three to four emails to find time for us to meet because it's time wasted.

Here is an example of an email with my scheduling link in the content.

Hi Kayla,

It was great meeting you on Thursday. I would appreciate a quick phone chat to discuss speaking at your company retreat. Please use my scheduling link [add a link to your scheduler] *to find a convenient time for us both.*

Using a scheduling system like Breely or Calendly to schedule meetings, particularly external meetings, offers several benefits:

Time Efficiency: It reduces back-and-forth in the scheduling process by eliminating the need for multiple emails or messages to find a suitable time. It makes the booking experience seamless for the client, and they can schedule at their convenience, even after hours. A simple link saves about 12 minutes of scheduling back-and-forth for each meeting. After five meetings, you've saved yourself about an hour!

Automatic Reminders: Sends reminders to participants, reducing no-shows or trying to find the link for the meeting.

Focus Time: Keeps blocks for focus time so people can't schedule over it. You can also pad time and not allow meetings back to back to give you time to make notes, refill your water, and still be on time for your next meeting. I have a padding of 15 minutes before and after all meetings. Cook Wealth, one of our consulting and training clients, began padding their meetings and realized it was a benefit *to their clients.* They could show up at every meeting ready to go and prepared instead of a little frazzled from rushing from the previous meeting. They also started blocking out time on their calendar for follow-ups from client calls. Before, they allowed big blocks of time for client calls without the time for them to do the work needed to serve those same clients.

Integrates calendars: Syncs with personal and team calendars to prevent double-booking.

Provides different meeting types: I have meeting links for different amounts of times and purposes. Some have forms attached, so I'm even more prepared for the call. For example, My Speaking and Training Connection call has a form to learn more about their event or company so I can be more prepared. My Coaching Discovery call has an application, which saves me time if I can tell it's not a good fit. It also saves them time by clarifying what they need before the call. I also have links for 25-minute virtual coffees and 10-minute virtual espressos. I keep my phone on *Do Not Disturb* almost all the time during work hours, so I'm not interrupted during a coaching session or speaking engagement, so having that 10-minute link saves a lot of frustration.

Take payments: Breely can even take payment for people who want a RaderCo Inbox Rescue package or laser coaching session. This is another way to make the transaction seamless: they can register, pay, and schedule all in one go!

Not everyone in your company may need a scheduling system, but it's especially helpful for salespeople, demo providers, customer support providers, onboarding professionals, interviewers, and consultants.

In essence, any role or department requiring frequent meetings or appointments can benefit from a scheduling system.

TL;DR

Consider using a scheduling system to schedule meetings if you're tired of the back-and-forth emails. These tools let others see your available time slots and book appointments directly, syncing with your calendar to avoid double-booking. They save time, send automatic reminders, and help you maintain focus by preventing back-to-back meetings. They especially benefit sales, customer support, HR, and consulting roles.

Implement Meeting-Free Days or Weeks

Want to go all in? Adopt Meeting-Free Days or Weeks! Imagine all the focused work you could get done. Many companies do this with excellent results. Some companies have implemented this and abused the concept. For example, I worked with one company that had meeting-free Fridays, but then people would say things like, "Let's meet on Friday since everyone will be available." It erodes trust and is deflating for team members.

TechSmith, a 300-person fully remote company, experimented with 30 days of no meetings and relied solely on asynchronous communication such as video screen capture, chat, and email. Over 15% of employees *strongly agreed* that they felt more productive. After the experiment, 85% of people were more thoughtful about whether a meeting had to be done and if the information could be shared asynchronously instead.[46]

---

[46] "Techsmith's Async-First Study Eliminated Meetings and Saw +15% Increase in Employee Productivity," Techsmith, January 10, 2023 (https://www.techsmith.com/press/latest/async-first-experiment/)

Shopify experimented with a two-week "cooling off" period from all meetings and did away with all recurring meetings with three or more people to start people off with a "clean slate" to determine if that meeting was really needed. They ruled that any meeting with more than 50 people, like an all-company meeting, had to be done within a six-hour window on Thursdays. They also have meeting-free Wednesdays for employees to do focused work.[47]

RaderCo client Abdo has two meeting-free weeks per year. Some team members choose to take vacation or days off during that time because they don't have Fear Of Missing Out (FOMO) when they return. Others choose it to work on special projects or simply do heads-down, deep work.

Personally, I only allow meetings three days per week. I don't meet on Fridays unless it's in person (the one exception to this rule is presentations or keynotes). I save those days for walkie-talkies or coffee dates.

Benefits of Meeting-Free Days or Weeks include:

Enhanced Focus: Employees can dedicate uninterrupted time to deep work, leading to increased productivity and quality of work.

Reduced Burnout: Less time spent in meetings can lower stress levels, promoting overall well-being.

---

[47]   Jennifer Korn, "This Tech Company is Clearing Out Recurring Meetings From Employee Calendars," CNN, January 3, 2023 (https://www.cnn.com/2023/01/03/tech/shopify-meetings/index. html)

Increased Efficiency: Teams can complete tasks faster without constant interruptions, streamlining project timelines.

Creativity Boost: Unstructured time allows for creative thinking and innovation, as employees have space to brainstorm and explore new ideas.

Empowerment: Trusting employees with their schedules fosters autonomy and ownership, boosting morale and engagement.

Improved Collaboration: When meetings are *necessary,* they become more focused and productive, enhancing collaboration and decision-making.

Meeting-free days or weeks can lead to a more motivated, productive, and creative workforce.

How can I implement it? Pilot one day a week to be meeting free. Survey your company to see which day they would prefer. One study showed that Monday is the least favorite meeting day (47%), followed by Friday (40%).[48] Incorporate a meeting-free week mid-summer when people may take a vacation, prepare for one, or return. If your company doesn't shut down, you could also implement this the week of Christmas to New Year's Day.[49]

---

[48] Chang Chen, "Shocking Meeting Statistics in 2021 That Will Take You By Surprise," Otter.AI, December 24, 2020 (https://otter.ai/blog/meeting-statistics)

[49] "Meeting Statistics: Effectiveness, Virtual Conferencing, and More in 2024," Teamstage (https://teamstage.io/21-monumental-meeting-statistics/)

Another option is to have video-free days where clients can opt not to be on video to decrease video fatigue and get a break from staring at the screen. Dropbox has implemented "Video-Free Fridays" as part of its work culture.

TL;DR

Boost productivity and happiness by adopting meeting-free days or weeks. This allows for deep work, reduces burnout, and increases efficiency. It's crucial to stick to the plan to maintain trust if implemented. Start with one meeting-free day per week and survey employees for their preferences. Incorporate meeting-free weeks around holidays or popular vacation time for maximum impact. Embrace this approach for a motivated, productive, and creative workforce.

References

Chang Chen, "Shocking Meeting Statistics in 2021 That Will Take You By Surprise," Otter.AI, December 24, 2020 (https://otter.ai/blog/meeting-statistics)

Barry Elad, "29+ Amazing Meeting Statistics 2023: Virtual vs. In-Person Meeting, Zoom, and Productivity," Enterprise Apps Today, October 4, 2023 (https://www.enterpriseappstoday.com/stats/meeting-statistics.html)

Jennifer Korn, "This Tech Company is Clearing Out Recurring Meetings From Employee Calendars," CNN, January 3, 2023 (https://www.cnn.com/2023/01/03/tech/shopify-meetings/index.html)

Stephanie, Mickelson, "How You Can Use Jeff Bezos' Two-Pizza Rule to Find Career and Financial Success,"

Yahoo Finance, April 24, 2024 (https://finance.yahoo.
com/news/jeff-bezos-two-pizza-rule-130039391.
html?guccounter=1&guce_referrer=aHR0cHM-
6Ly93d3cuZ29vZ2xlLmNvbS88&guce_referrer_
sig=AQAAAGOvjQ8kHCA8e4M8Qus8CVeuRo3m-
MksBFfKtEA32jSxNw0iuvcxPbgBWQrQN01Ou-
vMVRV6CM5mbwQzUPforA-ysy5TE666TLPCl-
4n67xyT8ue7cUdpBZYZUYuUCwB5g8guJ-h4VdV-
yVjTVaEEwLuemp161DpQmAkcEJuiGvY42vx)

Eric Moore, "31 Need-To-Know Meeting Statistics
(2023 Update): Virtual, Zoom, In-Person,
Productivity," Overheard on Conference Calls,
March 2, 2023 (https://overheardonconferencecalls.
com/business/meeting-statistics/)

Marcey Rader, "Embrace the Bottlenecks," RaderCo
(https://www.helloraderco.com/bottlenecks/)

Ola Svenson, "Are We All Less Risky and More
Skillful Than Our Fellow Drivers?," Acta
Psychologica, 1981 (https://web.archive.org/
web/20120722210701/http://heatherlench.com/
wp-content/uploads/2008/07/svenson.pdf)

"Meeting Cost Calculator," Otter.Ai, (https://
otter.ai/meeting-cost-calculator)

"Meeting Statistics: Effectiveness, Virtual Conferencing,
and More in 2024," Teamstage (https://teamstage.
io/21-monumental-meeting-statistics/)

"Techsmith's Async-First Study Eliminated Meetings and Saw +15% Increase in Employee Productivity," Techsmith, January 10, 2023 (https://www.techsmith. com/press/latest/async-first-experiment/)

"The Surprising Connection Between After-Hours Work and Decreased Productivity," Slack, December 5, 2023 (https://slack.com/blog/ news/the-surprising-connection-between-after-hours-work-and-decreased-productivity)

CHAPTER 4

TASK AND PROJECT MANAGEMENT

Welcome to the wild world of task and project management! Managing tasks and projects in today's fast-paced business landscape can often feel like a high-wire act without a safety net.

Fear not! This chapter is here to save you from the chaos. Think of this as your ultimate section to transforming the way your team works.

I'll show you how to prioritize like a pro, communicate like a champion, and streamline your processes so efficiently that even your Monday mornings will start to feel a little less, well, Monday-ish. You'll no longer go to sleep at night with the Sunday Scaries. Whether you're leading a tiny but mighty team or steering the ship of a large organization, the tips and strategies in this chapter will help you conquer your to-do list and keep your projects on track.

TL;DR

Master task and project management with tips to streamline processes, prioritize effectively, and keep your team on track. Say goodbye to chaotic Mondays.

Problems:

- **No Project Management System (PMS) or Task Management System (TMS):** The absence of structured systems makes tracking progress and assigning tasks difficult.

- **Lack of Prioritization:** When tasks aren't ranked by importance, it leads to confusion and inefficiency.

- **Poor Communication:** Deadlines and expectations aren't clearly communicated, resulting in missed deadlines and misunderstandings.

- **Task Overload:** Too many tasks overwhelm employees, leading to burnout and decreased productivity.

- **Ineffective Tools or Storage Repositories:** Time is wasted searching for information, and tools aren't user-friendly or integrated.

- **Bottlenecks:** Key information or resources are inaccessible, and cross-functional teams don't prioritize tasks equally.

- **Follow-up via Email:** Lack of a centralized system forces reliance on email for task follow-ups, causing clutter and inefficiency.

- **Not Looking Upstream:** The failure to identify and eliminate upstream inefficiencies impacts downstream tasks.

- **No Processes:** A lack of standardized procedures leads to inconsistent task management and execution.

Solutions:

- **PMS or TMS with Training:** Implement and train staff on a robust PMS/TMS to streamline task assignment and tracking.

- **Communication Process:** Establish clear protocols for assigning tasks and updating progress to ensure everyone is on the same page (i.e., putting all requests into your PMS instead of sending via chats).

- **Regular Review of Tasks and Projects:** Conduct frequent reviews to prioritize tasks and adjust plans as needed.

- **Monitor Workloads:** Implement regular feedback and check-ins to redistribute workloads and prevent burnout.

- **Project Plans with Timelines and Milestones:** Develop detailed project plans that include timelines, milestones, and contingency plans to ensure projects stay on track.

- **More Regular Performance Reviews:** Increase the frequency of performance reviews to provide timely feedback and address issues promptly.

- **Streamline Processes Upstream:** Identify and eliminate inefficiencies at the source to improve overall workflow.

- **Standardized Processes:** Develop and enforce standardized procedures for task management to ensure consistency and efficiency.

Levels

Action Steps for Individuals:
- Batch Your Tasks
- Create Theme Days
- Focus on Your Top Three

Action Steps for Managers:
- Consider Maker vs Manager
- Reflect, Prioritize, Plan

Action Steps for C+/Business Owners:
- Implement a Project Management System (PMS)

INDIVIDUAL

Batch Your Tasks

Batching your tasks is a huge timesaver. People often think about batching errands but rarely about batching their tasks. Doing all your errands in one chunk each week in an order that saves you time and money is really no different from saving up your project work to tackle on Mondays and Wednesdays.

Think about it: When you're craving a cookie, you don't get out all the ingredients, make one cookie, clean up everything, and put it all away. You make an entire batch at once to save time. We can do batches with our brains, too. By not switchtasking all the time, we are protecting our minds from decision fatigue and saving time by not opening and closing various programs all day.

For example, instead of signing into my website every time I want to add something, I save those tasks for one block per week and do them all at once. Of course, if I have a broken link or typo, I fix that immediately, but the maintenance and changes I want to make can be saved for later, so I'm not reopening my admin screen whenever I have a thought. I keep a running list of what I need to add in the notes section of my recurring task for *Website Updates.*

A study by Slack found that productive people are 1.6 times more likely to block time to complete specific tasks, 1.7 times more likely only to check email at specific times, and 2.2 times more likely to set focus timers.[50]

> *"I used to run my to-do list from my inbox, but I now use tasks, scheduled blocks of intense email processing, and have zero notifications enabled on my phone or computer. I am more productive and less stressed, and I look forward to my projects instead of being filled with dread." – Tatyana Blankenship, Associate Director of Maintenance, Beam Therapeutics*

The number one thing people can batch that they don't is… email! Email isn't something we react to. Play offense and batch it like a task. Schedule to go into your inbox x times a

---

[50] "The Surprising Connection Between After-Hours Work and Decreased Productivity," Slack, December 5, 2023 (https://slack.com/blog/news/the-surprising-connection-between-after-hours-work-and-decreased-productivity)

day, depending on your role (e.g., if you're a customer service representative, you may need to check email the entire time during your eight-hour shift, but if you're a research chemist, checking once in the morning and once in the afternoon may be enough), and process all your email and then *close it out.*

I was very reactive as a Clinical Lead and Operations Trainer. Later, I trained myself to process emails only four times a day. I didn't tell anyone for months because I feared getting into trouble. When my boss complimented me one day on my efficiency, I confessed and told her that I had only been answering emails four times a day. Instead of reprimanding me, she was impressed and asked me to teach our team what I was doing! And this, in a tiny way, began my career as a productivity trainer and coach. At RaderCo, we've had personal coaching clients who stopped being reactive and went down to checking email one to three times per day, and not a single person they worked with noticed!

Examples of tasks I batch:

- Bank reconciliation and bill paying
- Client check-ins
- Prospect and former client follow-ups
- Video recordings
- LinkedIn post creation and commenting
- Podcast episode recording

- Newsletter and blog writing
- Email

What are some easy things you can batch instead of opening programs, documents, or spreadsheets every time you think of them?

TL;DR

Batching tasks saves time and boosts productivity by grouping similar activities, like emails or updates, into focused blocks. This reduces constant switching and decision fatigue and helps you work more efficiently. Apply batching to tasks like bill paying, client check-ins, or writing to maximize your effectiveness.

Create Theme Days

Now that you have the batching of tasks down, go even further and create Theme Days. When you create Theme Days, you assign tasks to specific days of the week to create a theme. This way, your brain gets into that mode quickly, you don't have to think about what day you will do which task, and you are doing less switchtasking. Although I stick to Theme days as much as possible, my schedule varies, so I can't assign the same tasks on the same day every week. I'm not so rigid that I don't shuffle things as needed, but instead of switching from marketing to writing a presentation to working with a client and back to marketing, all in one afternoon, I save up most marketing tasks for one day of the week. I batch my tasks this way to make it easier for my brain by working on one type of activity at a time.

Having one day a week that you work on a specific type of task or if you are currently working on several projects, dividing those into different days as much as possible can keep you from getting thoughts mixed up. It will allow you to focus on one project at a time. This doesn't mean that if something comes up that needs to be addressed for *Project A* on Wednesday, which is your *Project B* day, you don't address it, but if it can wait until *Project A* day, then move it forward.

Here's an example of my themes as of the writing of this book. Because I travel for business, and I might be giving a corporate workshop or conference keynote some days, I shuffle things around if needed. But for the most part, I try to stick to my themes:

- **Monday** – Coach clients, professional development
- **Tuesday** – Coach clients, outreach, business development
- **Wednesday** – Coach clients, marketing
- **Thursday** – Presentations, content creation, finances, no meetings
- **Friday** – Face-to-face walking or coffee dates, admin, shipping, industry news

> *"I knew doing similar tasks together would naturally be more efficient. What I didn't expect was how much clarity, focus, and ultimately, peace Theme Days would bring to my daily work! Deciding that Tuesday morning is content marketing creation time or that Friday is internal communications day means I spend a lot less time thinking about how I should be spending my time—and a lot less time*

worrying that I'm not focused on the real priorities. Choosing Theme Days has felt like a weight lifted off my shoulders!" – Matt Bailey

TL;DR

Take task batching further with Theme Days—assign specific tasks to certain days of the week for better focus and less switchtasking. By grouping similar activities together, like marketing or client coaching, your brain quickly adapts, reducing the mental load and increasing productivity. While flexibility is key, sticking to themed days streamlines your workflow and keeps projects organized.

Focus on Your Top Three

It doesn't matter how many boxes are checked off that task list if the right boxes aren't being checked. Being busy and achieving the most tasks in one day doesn't make you a superstar. Knowing how to prioritize those tasks appropriately is critical to reaching your goals. Do you think Oprah Winfrey, Tim Cook, Warren Buffet, and Sheryl Sandberg are looking to check boxes all day? They didn't get where they are by getting the *most* things done. They got where they are, getting the *right* things done.

I call this the *Top Three Method*. Why only three? Turns out, our brains have a thing for threes. Ever notice how jokes, stories, and even speeches often center around sets of three? This phenomenon is known as the "Rule of Three," a principle suggesting that information presented in groups of three is more engaging and memorable.[51]

Information presented this way is:

1. **Brain-Friendly**: Three things are easier for our minds to handle and remember.

2. **Easily Recognized as Part of a Pattern**: Three is magic because it's the smallest number for creating recognizable patterns.

3. **Powerful for Focus**: Three items keep our attention without overwhelming us.

So, if you want something to stick, think in threes!

Besides, we really can't have more than three top priorities, and arguably, there is only one priority at a time—whatever you are doing *now*.

How to think about your Top Three:

I begin annually, but this may feel like too much or not work for your role. If you are "allergic" to this recommendation, you may also choose to have only one or two priorities. That works—just don't have more than three!

Annual—Spaceship View: I pick three priorities or themes, each personal and professional, to give a big-picture view.

---

[51] Gail Jefferson, "List-Construction as a Task and Resource," Studies in Ethnomethodology and Conversation Analysis, 1990 (https://liso-archives.liso.ucsb.edu/Jefferson/List%20construction.pdf)

Quarterly—Airplane View: On the last day of the quarter, I review my next 90 days to determine my *Top Three Priorities* for the next quarter.

Monthly—Skyscraper View: On the last day of each month, I jot down my *Top Three Priorities* for the following month.

Weekly—Treetop View: I decide on my *Top Three Priorities* for the next week on the last day of the work week or sometimes on Sundays.

Daily—Garden View: I decide on my 1-3 priorities for the next day at the end of each day.

I write my annual, quarterly, monthly, and weekly priorities on a giant rolling whiteboard in my office, so they always stare me in the face, making no excuses for forgetting or procrastinating. Having that whiteboard in front of me helps me determine what's essential for me to work on without any questions and makes me intentional about what's important. I also have my weekly Theme Days at the bottom of the board. I keep everything in my Powered Path Playbook® as well. My annual, quarterly, and monthly priorities also go into our project management system so my team can see them.

Why the month, week, or evening before? It's better to slide into your next work sprint knowing what needs to be done outside any moment of urgency (or procrastination). At the end of each workday, I schedule at least one of my *Top Three Tasks* for the next day. I recommend this instead of in the morning because you will end your day knowing exactly what you need to do tomorrow and won't spend your first 20-30 minutes planning your day (or, in some cases, procrastinating by planning). You also can go into your evening knowing the plan and feeling at ease. You won't be tempted to hit your inbox first (another person's agenda) before working on *your* agenda.

Consider the timing of those *Top Three Tasks* according to your energy levels and schedule for the day. As an early morning person, I do my most important task (the one I am most likely to avoid) first or when I know I will have uninterrupted focus time. If I'm going to be working during an airport layover or between client calls, I'll do things that I can quickly cross off my list with the minimal focus required. I don't do those things during long blocks that would be better spent doing deep work. If it's writing or creating, I will need complete silence and non-distracted time, and I will wait until I have a chunk of that kind of time available.

If you're more of an afternoon or evening person, you may need to "warm up" in the morning with your lighter tasks, but you have to be even more mindful of your schedule and whether meetings or other tasks will eat up your day.

No matter what time of day you are at your best, keep your first 30-60 minutes (longer if possible) *to yourself.* Don't hit your inbox first! Most people don't know exactly when you start work, so what does it matter if the email is answered at 8:00 a.m. or 8:30 a.m.? Do at least one task for yourself first, ideally, a Top Three Task.

Causes of procrastination can be dislike of the task, fear of doing a lousy job, fear of doing a good job (and getting rewarded with more work), or underestimating the time to do it. Procrastination can also be selfish. If someone expects something, you might unconsciously wield your control by withholding what they need. You might also be that adrenaline junkie that needs that rush of a deadline at the end. If you find a task that doesn't get done regularly, stop, evaluate, and resolve the why instead of constantly kicking it down your to-do list.

You may have heard about the *Eisenhower Method for Priority Order*. It separates tasks into four quadrants:

1. **Urgent and Important**—These tasks must be taken care of immediately. Either there is a crisis or a pressing deadline, or you have procrastinated too long, and they must be done now.

2. **Urgent but Not Important**—These are tasks that need to be done quickly and are associated with or assigned by someone else, or tasks where other people are waiting for you, and you can't be the bottleneck.

3. **Not Urgent, but Important**— These tasks help you move toward your goals and should be scheduled appropriately. If, however, you procrastinate, they can quickly move to Urgent and Important.

4. **Neither Important nor Urgent**—These tasks can be sent to the bottom of the list. They are "nice to have" or can be done during a light weekday. They may even be distractions and discarded altogether.

Think of your tasks and whether they are urgent or important. If they are both, it will be obvious which belongs in your top three and needs your attention.

ABC Delegate Eliminate

But Marcey, I have more than three tasks! Of course you do! The important thing is the priority order of those tasks and to look at your day with these questions in mind:

> *If I don't complete these three things, could they negatively impact the rest of my week or other scheduled tasks?*

> *If I were to go on vacation tomorrow, what would I need to do today so I could unplug?*

> *What would I need to focus on if my device had only 45 minutes of battery left?*

When reviewing all your tasks, identify and label your top three as Task A, Task B, and Task C. Then, see if there are any others you can D (delegate) and/or E (eliminate).

D – Delegate tasks where and when you can. If you have direct reports or an assistant, give them the skills, knowledge, and tools to take over that task and then *trust them with it.* Can you outsource to a service or hire a professional for a home task?

E – Eliminate other tasks. Skim through your tasks every day and determine if there is anything you can eliminate. We all have "nice to do" tasks, but eliminate them if the timing isn't right because you're in the middle of a project or have things going on at home. Seeing that task being moved forward day after day will do nothing but remind you that, once again, you didn't get to something. Stop doing it if your client or company wouldn't pay you your hourly wage for the two hours you spend formatting that spreadsheet perfectly. If you are thinking of creating a report that no one asked for but you think might be helpful and would take 30 minutes, eliminate it, at least for now. Our careers and lives have seasons for "nice to do." But if you are in a season of overload or overwhelm, don't even put it on the list or set a deadline; if you haven't done it by X date, it just gets deleted.

> Are there any tasks you repeatedly push forward to the next day over and over again? If so, they probably don't need to be done—chuck 'em. Evaluating your tasks is good practice to determine if they are still a priority.
>
> Karyn, a CFO client, had a long list of things she wanted to get done but never found the time. I asked her to create a deadline, which she set for Christmas. Anything that didn't get done by then was deleted. She added things to her "Christmas list," and when she found extra time in her schedule, she would go to it and see what she could check off. However, by Christmas, that list had to be gone.

Focusing and concentrating on a task only works if you can discriminate. It doesn't do any good to be focused if you are spending that time on irrelevant or "outside your zone of genius" tasks.

> *"Before implementing ABC Delegate Eliminate and identifying three essential items the night before, I dealt daily with a mile-long list that seemed to never get smaller. And my afternoon was spent wallowing*

in "*I will never make progress on this list, and it will be moved to tomorrow, which will likely be worse. Is there anything I can check off to call this day any part of a success?*" *Of course, I could only work on quick things with that perspective, so it became self-fulfilling. I went home most days discouraged and rarely felt the feeling of accomplishment I was looking for. After about two weeks of doing ABC almost every day, I have checked off more and ended more days feeling accomplished than I had in months prior. Today, I'm going home before 4 p.m. (typically 5:30 or later). I already checked off some of tomorrow's list because my top three were done by 2:30 p.m. Plus I know (because I worked the list last night) that there's nothing more important there.*" – Eric Syfrett, CPA, CFO, Executive Pastor

Special note

Throughout my 20s and 30s, I prioritized the wrong "more" at the expense of my relationship with my husband and my health. I triggered a preventable condition called hypothalamic amenorrhea (HA), which affects approximately 1.6 million women, and I didn't have a menstrual cycle *for 12 years*. I always thought I could make up for lost time after getting that promotion, finishing that project, or making a certain amount of money. I was wrong. I go into more detail in my TEDx talk: "The Relentless Pursuit of More: The High Cost of High Achievement." You can view it here: www.marceyrader.com/tedx

> Your health and relationships are more important than anything and should always be included in your Top Three personal priorities.

TL;DR

The Top Three Method prioritizes your most important tasks, helping you focus on what truly matters. Limiting your top priorities to three boosts productivity and prevents you from feeling overwhelmed. Use ABC Delegate Eliminate to handle less critical tasks. Remember, health and relationships should always be part of your top personal priorities.

MANAGER

Consider Maker vs Manager

In July 2009, Paul Graham wrote a blog post called "Maker's Schedule, Manager's Schedule" that has become famous in productivity circles, especially among tech giants.[52] I share a snapshot below, but I encourage you to read the short post.

Snapshot:

Programmers, coders, scientists, researchers (and other *makers*) dislike meetings because they work on a different schedule than managers. Makers need large, uninterrupted blocks of time to be productive, while managers can operate

---

[52] Paul Graham, "Maker's Schedule, Manager's Schedule," July 2009 (https://paulgraham.com/makersschedule.html)

on an hour-by-hour schedule. A single meeting can disrupt a maker's entire day, whereas it's just another task for a manager. Understanding these different schedules can help those who set up meetings minimize the impact on others' focus time.

Making your team operate on a manager's schedule when they are makers is very disruptive, causes them to take more time to complete tasks, and can contribute to mistakes. It is crucial to allow your makers to block off time every week to "make or create." It's also essential for *you* to block this time off. Whether it's one full or half day that you have email and chat shut down entirely and no meetings scheduled, this will allow you to focus on essential tasks that require more concentration. You can save up work for that day and know you will be able to complete it. Fifteen minutes here and 30 minutes there won't cut it. And if you're saving up your "real work" for nighttime when the kids are in bed, your brain is tired, and you are now sacrificing sleep.

Everyone needs time to focus without interruption. For my meeting-heavy corporate clients, I schedule at least one hour a day with no interruptions on most days, if not every day of the week. Decide ahead of time what your most intensive tasks are for that week and schedule yourself to work on them.

What if you allow your team to work email, chat, and meeting free for the first hour of every day? You could also extend it to include the last hour of their day. Encourage them to schedule "make and create" time to get more done using less energy.

TL;DR

Makers need uninterrupted time, while managers work in an hourly cadence. Forcing makers onto a manager's schedule disrupts productivity and increases errors. Block dedicated "make time" each week, and schedule at least an hour daily for focused work without interruptions. This boosts efficiency and reduces burnout.

Reflect, Prioritize, Plan

We don't learn anything from our experiences if we don't intentionally reflect on them consistently. I've been using a methodology since 2012 that we call the Powered Path Program™ of Reflection, Prioritizing, and Planning. The key is the reflection piece. Doing these reflections with at least one trusted peer, a manager, or a direct report is critical. You get so much value from their questions, feedback, and comments. Reflections, prioritizing, and planning occur with annual, quarterly, monthly, weekly, and daily prompts like Big Win, Smartest Decisions, and What I Would Have Done Differently.

This falls under the Manager category because we heard too many managers say they didn't know how to lead a one-to-one conversation and direct reports saying they couldn't remember their accomplishments by the time their annual review rolled around. This method trains team members to manage and drive the meeting.

> *"One of the biggest mistakes people make is assuming their manager knows everything they have been doing and the value of it. It's up to you to clearly explain to your manager what projects you are*

working on, the obstacles you have overcome, the specific actions you took, and the results you have achieved. I believe it's important to have regular check-ins with your manager throughout the year where you keep your manager updated on these things. And write them down! Don't wait until it's performance management time to try remembering everything—you won't be able to. Keep a running list, especially when you start a new project, hit a new obstacle, or achieve a specific result." – Jennifer McCluskey, RaderCo Career Specialist

The Powered Path Program™ is an online microlearning course with 30 seconds to four minutes long modules, which takes around an hour. The Powered Path Playbook® is a template for managers and their team to keep them on the same page for priorities and tracking goals and outcomes. Since *Lessons Earned* and *What Didn't Work Well* are two of the prompts, they encourage people to share their "oopsies," which often results in personal and professional growth. It also shows that we *expect* them to work outside their comfort zone and sometimes fail at a task. If everything works perfectly all the time, we're probably not challenging ourselves enough. You can learn more about the program at helloraderco.com/playbook.

You can also develop your own template of questions that includes tracking accomplishments and lessons so that when annual review time rolls around, no one is left scrambling to remember what they did nine months ago.

"The Powered Path Playbook® enables me to really think hard about my big picture goals and then funnel them down to what I need to do in the short term

to achieve those long-term goals. It's so empowering because it helps me see that the little actions I'm taking, mundane and tedious as they might be day to day, are leading to a bigger goal. I've tried over a half a dozen different productivity tools, and none of them has worked. This actually works for me, and I plan to continue using it." – Christian Cherniawski, Publishing Success Strategist, SelfPublishing.com

TL;DR

The Powered Path Program™ emphasizes reflection, prioritizing, and planning to track growth and accomplishments. Regular reflection with a peer or manager aids in effective one-to-ones and annual reviews. The program offers a structured template to support this process, promoting learning from both successes and failures. Learn more at helloraderco.com/playbook.

C+/BUSINESS OWNER

Implement a Project Management System (PMS)

Do you feel like no matter how many hacks you employ and announcements you send, your company will never get out of email hell? There is a reason why you may never break free. It's because you're trying to manage projects out of the inbox instead of using a project management system (PMS).

At RaderCo, we are often hired to help companies drowning in their inboxes. Well, I have a secret for you. We are not miracle workers. We don't have magic fairy dust to sprinkle on your inbox to remove all your woes. And between you, me, and the interwebs, your company will never get out of its inbox if you don't use some kind of project management system (PMS).

> *"Using your inbox for managing your tasks is like being a firefighter, constantly putting out fires as they flare up. If you embrace a task management system, you're more of an architect of your job. Every task in the system has a place, purpose, and deadline, allowing you to build toward your goals." – Rijul Arora, RaderCo Digital Wellness and Microsoft Team Specialist*

A PMS is a program like ClickUp (our preferred PMS), Asana, Trello, Monday, Jira, Notion, or a similar tool that tracks all the tasks within a project. It may also host resources, documents, and videos.

When companies use a project management system, there is no emailing back and forth for status requests, information sharing, and check-ins. Employees often have access to a PMS and don't even realize it.

> *"Companies need to train their staff on how to use their current tools at more than a basic level. I'm often asked "Is there an app for that?" Many times they have access to a tool already and simply don't know about the function they are looking for." – Judith Guertin, RaderCo Productivity Specialist*

Problems:

- **Scattered Information**: Important project details get lost in a flood of emails.

- **Lack of Centralization**: There's no single source for project status, deadlines, or task assignments that everyone can see.

- **Email Overload:** Team members struggle to keep track of project-related information.

- **Delayed Responses**: Critical updates and discussions can be buried, causing delays.

- **Poor Accountability**: Without clear task assignments, knowing who is responsible for what is difficult.

- **Lack of Tracking**: Progress on tasks and projects is harder to monitor, increasing the risk of missed deadlines.

- **Fragmented Document Sharing**: Files and documents are often shared piecemeal via email, making collaboration cumbersome.

- **Manual Follow-ups**: More time is spent manually tracking tasks and sending reminders.

- **Redundant Effort**: There's an increased likelihood of duplicated work and missed tasks due to poor visibility.

- **No Real-time Insights**: It's harder to gather real-time data on project progress, hindering informed decision-making.

- **Difficulty in Identifying Issues**: Spotting and addressing problems early becomes challenging without proper tracking and reporting.

Solutions:

- **Centralized Information**: Keeps all project-related data in one place, reducing the risk of losing important information in overflowing inboxes.

- **Task Tracking**: Allows you and your team to assign tasks, set deadlines, and track progress.

- **Team Communication**: Facilitates seamless communication among team members, with discussion threads and comments directly linked to tasks.

- **Document Sharing**: Allows easy sharing and collaboration on documents and files within the project context.

- **Automated Reminders**: Automatically sends reminders and updates, reducing the need for follow-up emails.

- **Time Management**: Helps manage time and resources more effectively by visualizing project timelines and workloads.

- **Clear Ownership**: Assigns clear responsibility for tasks, making it easier to hold team members accountable.

- **Progress Tracking**: Real-time updates on project status help identify bottlenecks and ensure timely completion.

- **Reporting**: Provides insights and analytics on project performance, making it easier to make informed decisions.

- **Improvement**: Identifies areas for improvement through detailed reports and feedback.

ALERT! Microsoft Teams, Slack, and your inbox are NOT project management tools.

Those tools do not assign dates, delegate, or prioritize. They are for communication and distraction (depending on how you use them). If you want to know what's happening with a project across teams or departments, track smaller projects and tasks within a larger project, or assign priorities and responsibilities, these things should happen within a project management system.

At RaderCo, we rarely email each other internally. There may be two or three emails a month, and that's only because an external client has emailed us and we are copying a team member. When we get an email that is a task, we forward it to ClickUp to prioritize and give a due date, assign it to a specific person, and mark it complete when it's done. I don't need to check in with anyone about a task because I can see in ClickUp if it's in progress or completed.

We host all how-to videos, agendas, and documents in ClickUp and use it for our Client Relationship Management System.

And oh boy, do we have templates! Whenever I get a speaking engagement, a new coaching client, or write a podcast episode or article, I select a template within the system. Every task associated with that project auto-populates with the task's name, the person it is assigned to, and the date it needs to be done. Yes, ClickUp *even maps out the dates* based on how many days I've determined it needs to be done from the master task date.

> *"Using a project management system is a game changer for my ADHD. I never worry about missing*

*tasks or updates—everything's in one place. No
internal emails, no redundancy. We share pages,
docs, forms, and even make video/audio recordings
for quick clarity. Real-time task updates eliminate
constant check-ins, and urgent needs are handled
with a simple tag. I love it!" – Lisa Wood, RaderCo
Client Concierge and Marketing Specialist*

We can help you decrease your email and give you strategies
to reduce your anxiety around checking all the time. We can
help train your team members around those ever-popular
"reply alls" (which wouldn't happen in a PMS) or "Thanks!"
emails. We can show you shortcuts and settings adjustments
to streamline your email processing and workflow. Still, we
cannot shift your company culture to live outside the inbox
without the help of a PMS.

While it may seem daunting, if you expect your company to
grow, it won't become any easier without this tool. If you're
nervous about implementing a company-wide system, start
with one team to pilot a system. Choosing a more siloed team
that could learn to work within it together is smart. Then, add
on the team that they work with most often so you can see
how it works cross-functionally. Then, embrace it across the
department and, eventually, the whole company.

And for the love of pizza, hire someone to set it up and train
you on it! I can't count how often I've consulted with a company
that paid a ton of money for a tool but expected their internal
staff to learn it while setting it up themselves or didn't hire
an expert to train their staff. One of the best investments I've
ever made was hiring a ClickUp consultant to set my company
up. I still spent over 40 hours in one quarter writing all the

processes, creating task templates, and doing the training, but it was so worth it as we have had people on and offboard. And when you consider that you'll likely be using this tool for years to come, the time spent setting things up feels even more worthwhile.

> *"Unfortunately, it's common for companies to invest in new software without a plan to provide proper training and resources. Many organizations assume that the new applications are intuitive, so employees will figure things out as they go, or they underestimate the time and support needed to use the software effectively. This can lead to poor adoption, mistakes, and missed opportunities to get the full value out of the investment." – Dawn Bjork, RaderCo Software Specialist*

TL;DR

Stuck in email hell or jail? Break free with a project management system. Start small, pilot with one team, and expand. Hire a professional to set it up and train your staff for the best results. It's never too late to tame the beast.

References

Paul Graham, "Maker's Schedule, Manager's Schedule," July 2009 (https://paulgraham.com/makersschedule.html)

Gail Jefferson, "List-Construction as a Task and Resource," Studies in Ethnomethodology and Conversation Analysis, 1990 (https://liso-archives.liso.ucsb. edu/Jefferson/List%20construction.pdf)

"The Surprising Connection Between After-Hours Work and Decreased Productivity," Slack, December 5, 2023 (https://slack.com/blog/news/the-surprising-connection-between-after-hours-work-and-decreased-productivity)

SOS
REVIEW NEEDED!

It's Marcey dropping in one more time with a commercial break. Thank you for reading this far! High-fives and fist-bumps! I wanted to remind you to leave an honest review on Amazon and/or Goodreads. It's like giving my book a little magic boost in the world of words.

I'd love to hear your thoughts if you've got two minutes to spare (or the time it takes to schedule your day in your project management system). Whether you loved it, liked it, or even had a "meh" moment, your feedback helps other readers decide if it's worth the read. Bonus high fives if you write one thing you changed because of the book in your review!

reclaimyourworkday.com/amazon
reclaimyourworkday.com/goodreads
Thanks a million!

CHAPTER 5

REMOTE AND HYBRID WORK

Remote work has transformed how we approach our careers, offering unparalleled flexibility and opportunities. Once a niche option, it's now mainstream. However, it has its challenges.

I've worked remotely since 2001 and, at the peak, managed 18 people remotely and up to six people in different countries. I'd been training people how to work well remotely for over a decade, so when the pandemic pushed everyone into their houses without warning, I had more work than I could handle. Had I made the time—or foreseen the future—it would have been worthy of a case study to see what companies fared well, which companies sank, and analyze why. I would have checked in with an all-company survey at the six-month, one-year, and two-year mark.

Anecdotally, when I speak with managers at those companies and others when I deliver workshops on the topics "Work Well Remotely: Healthy Habits at Home" and "Manage Well Remotely: Lead Your Team Through the Screen," I run up against cognitive dissonance. Managers are too quick to say their workers aren't as productive at home. They can't imagine that the management style or culture needs to shift or that, indeed, their teams ARE more productive when working from home. The key to successfully managing a remote or hybrid team is to dump the fixed mindset about how everyone works better in the office, take off the hat of cognitive dissonance, and stop assuming that if there's a problem, it must be the fault of the remote worker.

The benefits of remote work are clear. Companies have reported increased productivity, reduced overhead costs, and access to a broader talent pool.[53] Employees enjoy the flexibility to balance personal and professional commitments, leading to higher job satisfaction.[54] However, remote work does have its challenges. The blurred lines between work and home, isolation, and constant distractions can diminish productivity and well-being for some individuals. Managers face hurdles in maintaining visibility, fostering communication, and keeping teams engaged. Companies must grapple with heightened security risks, preserve culture, and ensure technological reliability.[55]

---

[53] Nicholas Bloom, "How working from home works out," Stanford Institute for Economic Policy Research, June 2020 (https://siepr.stanford.edu/publications/policy-brief/how-working-home-works-out)

[54] Luciana Paulise, "The 2022 Status of Remote Work and Top Future Predictions," Forbes, December 8, 2022 (https://www.forbes.com/sites/lucianapaulise/2022/12/08/the-2022-status-of-remote-work-and-top-future-predictions/)

[55] "Remote, controlled—This changes everything: Five key actions companies can take now to operationalize their remote work program," Deloitte, December 12, 2022 (https://www.deloitte.com/global/en/about/press-room/deloitte-remote-controlled.html)

The hybrid model—a blend of remote and in-office work—seems to be a compromise. But hybrid work can come with its own set of challenges. Most workers appreciate having some in-office time, but it can be harder to figure out how to manage the work and projects when you're splitting your time between home and the workplace. Companies also have to figure out logistics so that those teams and individuals who most often collaborate in person are set up to do so. In light of these challenges, companies are rethinking office spaces and investing in technologies to support a distributed workforce.[56] The focus is on creating flexible work environments that adapt to future disruptions.

When planning out your week as a hybrid worker, if you know that you're less productive from a task perspective or have a more challenging time concentrating in the office, schedule your "quiet, focus tasks" for when you're at home and your less brain-intensive tasks for in the office. Always schedule in a buffer, knowing that you may have more "drive-bys" to your desk or people stopping to chat or ask questions in the office. Also, consider who you want to collaborate with in the office and schedule face time with them.

Entire books have been written just for remote and hybrid work. Here, I'm highlighting only a few things each role can do to improve the experience and crush it in their work culture.

---

[56] Ryan Ray M. Reyes, "Hybrid Work: From 'new' to 'now' normal," PWC, July 4, 2024 (https://www.pwc.com/ph/en/tax/tax-publications/taxwise-or-otherwise/2024/hybrid-work-from-new-to-now-normal.html)

TL;DR

Remote work, now mainstream, offers flexibility and productivity but also brings challenges like isolation and blurred work-life boundaries. Since 2001, my experience working with and managing remote teams has shown significant benefits. Companies thrive with increased productivity and reduced costs yet face hurdles in maintaining culture and security. Hybrid work mitigates these issues, but maintaining culture, security, and engagement remains tough.

Problems:

- **Isolation**: Lack of social interaction can lead to loneliness and reduced team unity.

- **Distractions**: Home environments have uncontrollable interruptions like family and pets.

- **Improper set-up:** Many remote workers use non-ideal spaces like kitchen tables or couches, making focus more difficult and leading to health problems from poor ergonomics.

- **Boundaries**: Separating work from personal life is tough, risking burnout.

- **Visibility**: Monitoring performance and ensuring accountability remotely can be difficult, leading to the fear of not getting promoted or seen for one's work. Fully remote workers are promoted 31% less frequently than in-office workers.[57] *This is not the same for hybrid workers.*

- **Physical Movement:** More sedentary lifestyles at home affect health.

- **Management:** Managers may over-communicate due to a lack of visibility on performance, which can put workers on edge.

- **Always-On:** Both managers and workers feel the need to always be available.

- **Communication:** Misunderstandings rise without face-to-face cues.

- **Hybrid Issues:** Split teams face fragmented communication and unequal information access.

- **Meetings:** Video fatigue and coordination issues make hybrid meetings less effective.

- **Engagement**: Keeping team morale and connection high is challenging.

- **Security:** Employees working remotely can increase the risk of data breaches and cybersecurity issues.

- **Culture**: Preserving company culture and values remotely is challenging.

- **Technology**: Ensuring all employees have reliable access to the necessary tools and platforms can be challenging.

---

[57] Margaret Faso, "Study Finds Fully Remote Work Leads to Fewer Promotions," HR Policy Association, January 19, 2024 (https://www.hrpolicy.org/insight-and-research/resources/2024/hr_workforce/public/01/study-finds-fully-remote-work-leads-to-fewer-promo)

Solutions:

- **Isolation:** Schedule regular, non-mandatory, virtual social events and encourage check-ins and team-building activities.

- **Distractions:** Designate a specific workspace at home and set guardrails with family during work hours.

- **Proper Set-Up:** Invest in ergonomic office furniture. Offer stipends for home office improvements.

- **Guardrails:** Establish clear work hours and stick to them. Use tools to manage notifications and time.

- **Visibility:** Schedule regular one-to-one meetings. Document and share accomplishments frequently.

- **Physical Movement:** Encourage regular breaks, exercise, and screen-free lunches. Implement wellness programs and benefits for remote employees.

- **Management:** Train managers on remote leadership skills. Focus on outcomes, *not activity monitoring or response time to emails and chats.*

- **Always-On:** Set clear expectations for availability. Promote healthy work-life integration.

- **Communication:** Use multiple channels (video, chat, email) with clear guidance on what to use and when. Train teams on effective virtual communication.

- **Hybrid Issues:** Standardize communication protocols. Ensure all team members have equal access to information.

- **Engagement:** Foster an inclusive and supportive remote culture by recognizing and rewarding contributions regularly.

- **Security:** Implement robust cybersecurity measures. Train employees on best practices for data security.

- **Culture:** Regularly communicate company values and Include remote workers in company events. Example: Having an in-person Summer Snack Hour with ice cream? Send your remote employees a $10 gift card to a local ice cream shop.

- **Technology:** Provide necessary tools and platforms. Ensure reliable IT support for remote employees.

Levels

Action Steps for Individuals:
- Set-Up Your Remote Office
- Communicate Family Guardrails
- Create Transitions To and From Work

Action Steps for Managers:
- Dump Productivity Paranoia
- Incorporate Virtual Team Building

Action Steps for C+/Business Owners:
- Trust in Your Remote Workforce
- Cultivate a Culture of Inclusion

INDIVIDUAL

Set-Up Your Remote Office

Your remote office set-up can be a game changer for motivation, inspiration, focus, concentration, and health. While I understand some people have limited space and no choice but to work from their kitchen tables or even their bedrooms, incorporating even one or two of these ideas can boost your Health-Powered Productivity™. Fortunately, I have a room dedicated to my office and virtual studio. As a speaker, I have a whole remote set-up, including three monitors (or five when I'm presenting), a microphone, headphones, a rolling whiteboard, an adjustable standup desk, a bike desk, and a portable standing desk. You can see my setup at helloraderco. com/virtual-speaking-home-office/.

Items to consider for a Health-Powered, Productive Office:

- **Standing or Sit-Stand Desk:** I go into more detail in Chapter 7 about why and how to use a standing desk, so I'll focus on the logistics here. You could get a large adjustable standing desk for your home office or a portable standing desk if you like moving around. I'm writing on a portable standing desk right now! I travel with it, take it to coffee shops, and have gifted one to our concierge and even a few clients. You could use it for specific tasks, take it outside when the weather is nice, or move it to a different location in your house when the kids come home. It's also nice to share with other household members and get your kids used to standing. Mine is a collapsible desk from Amazon that costs $25.

- **Anti-Fatigue Mat:** A desk mat can help prevent leg fatigue, regardless of your floor type. I've tested several and settled on a simple "kitchen sink" mat that chefs use in restaurants. I replace it once a year.

- **Anti-fatigue slippers**: I use the Kitin Parasole brand, along with my anti-fatigue mat, and there is a noticeable difference in how my legs feel at the end of the day.

- **Ergonomic chair or stool:** Sitting slumped over on your couch may work for 30 minutes, but you can't work like that for hours and days on end. Invest in a chair or stool that promotes good posture and can be alternately used with your standing desk.

- **A Second Screen or External Monitor**: Believe it or not, this has pros and cons. Often, people feel like they can't work without their second screen, but it can also lead to more distractions if you have that second monitor up all day with email and chat and use the other one to "work" from. That's not the right way to use them! Instead, use two monitors when you need two programs or have two documents you need to see simultaneously. Example: When creating a presentation, I have the client Productivity and Health Scorecard results and notes from my planning session on one screen and the slide deck on the other. This makes sense. I don't have my email on one and the slide deck on the other. When writing a blog post or working on this book, I take my laptop to a different place in the house or go somewhere else entirely because it's too easy to get distracted by the other monitor and try to multitask (which isn't effective!).

- **Ergonomic mouse:** This can't be understated. A mouse that fits well in your hand can save you from carpal tunnel and other arm, shoulder, back, and neck problems. I loved my Evoluent Vertical ergonomic mouse and used it for over a decade until Apple stopped supporting the software (I'm still hopeful they'll bring it back!). I now use an Apple Magic Trackpad, which feels better than a regular mouse. Test out a few options (Amazon has an excellent return policy). The goal: You shouldn't feel pain or fatigue at the end of the day.

- **Microphone:** Investing in a good microphone ensures your voice is heard clearly and often provides noise-canceling features. My husband can vacuum outside my office door, but my clients won't hear it.

- **Headphones:** Noise-canceling headphones reduce background noise, helping you concentrate. At this moment, a mower is going outside and people are talking. I just put my headphones on and kept on writing! High-quality headphones also help you hear others clearly during virtual meetings and keep your calls private. I don't like it when I'm speaking to people without headphones and know other people are in their house. Even if what I'm talking about isn't confidential, it makes me feel anxious and self-conscious (is someone off-camera listening to me?). Good headphones also need to be comfortable. If they give you a headache by the third hour of your day or your ears are sore, find a pair that fits your beautiful big or small head. And please, for the love of coffee-shop lattes, wear headphones in a public place, whether on a call or watching a video! Do not use your computer or phone speaker!

- **Webcam:** If you have a newer computer, they are now so good, you probably don't even need an external webcam; however, if you are using an external monitor, or ergonomically it isn't appealing, or the angle isn't great, invest in an external webcam. High-definition video will enhance your image beyond the filters video platforms provide. They will also perform better in various lighting conditions. I use a DSLR camera as my webcam, have a backup webcam, and have one on my computer (but I'm a speaker, so I always need to be prepared for technical difficulties!).

- **Whiteboard:** I have a rolling, double-sided whiteboard that lists my priorities for the week, month, quarter, and year, along with my daily themes. I also have whiteboard decals that I put on my wall and can cut to fit the size I need. At one point, I had a big 6' x 8' section of my office wall covered with whiteboard decals, and once they stopped fully erasing and my marker left stains, I simply peeled them off and put up new ones.

- **Door hanger or visible sign:** A sign alerts your family that you are in a meeting or in "concentration mode" and are not to be disturbed. When using this tool, remember to be consistent. Don't use it when you *can* be interrupted. It loses meaning if you hang it up all day and allow yourself to be interrupted.

- **Blue-Ray Blocking Glasses:** If you work on a computer, blue-ray-blocking glasses can protect your eyes and help with eye fatigue. You can get these with your prescription as an add-on, or if you don't need to wear glasses for vision, you can purchase glasses that gamers wear.

- **Natural light:** Get as much as you can!
- **Wi-Fi Extender:** A Wi-Fi extender, range extender, or repeater amplifies and extends the coverage of your existing Wi-Fi network. It can extend to parts of your house where WiFi is spotty or where you have a dead zone. We have one, so I can use my laptop on my porch and deck.

TL;DR

Your remote office setup can significantly boost motivation and productivity. Even with limited space, incorporating one or two essential items can enhance your work environment. Key items include a sit-stand desk, ergonomic chair, ergonomic mouse, quality microphone, noise-canceling headphones, high-definition webcam, whiteboard, blue-light blocking glasses, and a Wi-Fi extender. These tools help create a more efficient and comfortable remote workspace.

Communicate Family Guardrails

Working from home can be a productivity goldmine—no colleagues dropping by to distract you or aid in your procrastination, no breakroom cake temptations. You can throw a load of laundry in or start your dishwasher in the time it would take you to go across the office and use the public restroom. Studies have shown that remote employees often extend their workdays, sometimes *by as much as 48.5 minutes longer each day,* leading to nearly 200 additional hours per year—and this is *productive* time, not time they are making up because they got distracted during the day. This trend is supported by data from the National Bureau of Economic Research and studies by organizations like Ergotron and Owl Labs, highlighting increased productivity and better work-life balance among remote workers. More employees feel greater productivity at home than in the office.[58]

But let's face it, home has its distractions, too. Family and pets can also be a challenge. Non-remote family members may not understand that "working from home" means actual work. Use visible signs to indicate when you can't be disturbed. I use a door hanger during calls, presentations, or my first 90 minutes in the morning. That's Marcey Morning Magic time. I don't use it when doing admin-type tasks, nor do I keep it on all day (because I wouldn't be in deep work mode all day in the office either). This way, my husband knows when to interrupt me if he wants to say "good morning," ask me a question, or show me a video I "have to see." He knows I'm serious because I don't use it when I'm not in deep work mode or on a call. If you don't have a door, get creative—one woman uses a Wonder Woman cape, another a Concentration Crown, and one guy rocks bright red noise-canceling headphones. Have young kids who can't read a sign? Josh Elmore used a door hanger with R2D2 on one side and Chewbacca on the other. His little guy knew he was allowed inside when he saw Chewbacca.

---

[58] Gleb Tsipursky, PhD, "The Surprising Truth About Remote Work Productivity," Psychology Today, April 4, 2023 (https://www. psychologytoday.com/intl/blog/intentional-insights/202303/ the-surprising-truth-about-remote-work-productivity)

One gentleman in my Work Well Remotely training does a funny little routine and walks a lap around his kitchen to signal to his family that he's now "commuting to work" and can't be disturbed. Because it's so creative and he's consistent, they respect it and leave him alone.

> "Even as my kids get older and become more independent during the after-school hours, I prioritize taking a short break when they arrive home from school. Actions speak louder than words, and I want my boys to see me prioritizing my relationship with them over work. I've learned this is a place where quality is more important than quantity: a five-minute break where I can hug them, be fully present when asking about their school day, and simply check to ask if they will need my time or help later in the evening serves as an investment in the relationship while not compromising my afternoon work productivity. Proactively scheduling in the break minimizes getting interrupted later in the afternoon!" – Elisabeth Galperin, RaderCo Productivity Specialist

Sharing your calendar can also help. My husband knows my schedule and when I'm free for lunch. No shared calendar? Print your daily schedule or use a whiteboard to mark your breaks and end-of-day time. This also encourages you to stick to a schedule. My client Amy would tell her family what time she was closing down on Fridays. It kept her accountable for closing out and focusing on her family instead of doing "just one more thing."

As a remote worker, it's easy to slide into "disrespecting" the role. Unless your company allows you to take pets to the office, be very mindful of your animal interactions, especially when on screen. Your cat may think your laptop is an excellent spot for a nap, but not everyone on Zoom agrees. Keep untrained pets out of the office to maintain a professional vibe and not be distracting to others.

TL;DR

Working from home boosts productivity by avoiding office distractions, but it also has its own interruptions, like chores and family. Use signs or creative signals to show when you can't be disturbed, share your schedule, and set clear boundaries. Maintain professionalism by managing pets during meetings. Stay focused and maximize flexibility.

Create Transitions To and From Work

People who work from home tend to work longer hours and find it hard to disconnect. There are blurred boundaries because our work is always there and accessible. We feel like we need to be reactive to prove that we are working. We're afraid to even step away for lunch for 15-30 minutes, even though if we were in the office, we might go out with a colleague for an hour. We start work earlier and end later because even though we worked a full day or completed all of our tasks, no one has "seen" us do it, so we feel the pressure to always be on. With 24/7 digital communication tools, we may also be expected to be available longer. The lack of a routine of leaving the house and returning home can blur those lines. When going into the office, we change our clothes, maybe do our hair and makeup, commute, and then when we leave, we commute back, maybe change our clothes, and we're *home*.

Remote workers can mimic these start-and-stop transitions, which can be a breakthrough if you struggle to disconnect from work. Creating these lines between work and family life is also a sign that your family and your mental and physical health are priorities.

Morning Transitions

First of all, don't wake up with your manager! Giving up your morning to your company tells your brain that work is a priority over your health and family. If you were going to the office, you would give yourself an hour or more to get ready and commute, right? Why not use that time to exercise, have breakfast or a coffee, tend to your house or kids, and then start work? Who says you must check your email immediately just because you can? Your inbox is another person's agenda, and starting your day that way can totally derail any resolutions or behaviors you're trying to adopt.

Exercise: Morning exercisers tend to be more consistent, most likely because they aren't putting out fires, fighting against willpower after a long day, or feeling pulled by other priorities. Even if you aren't a morning exerciser, give yourself some type of movement in the morning, a movement snack,[59] if you will, so that you've at least gotten something in.

---

[59] Marcey Rader, "Why snackable Moments are Your New Productivity Hack," RaderCo https://www.helloraderco.com/snackable-moments/

Have a Start Time: No one knows when you start work until that first email or chat is sent (unless you keep a timesheet, and even then, they aren't looking at it right away). It often doesn't matter if you start at 7:30 a.m. or 8:30 a.m. Take that first half or full hour to do your top task, then go to your inbox or check your chat messages. A consistent start time may also be easier for your team and manager if they know your work hours.

Get dressed: Yes, even if it's only dressed up from the chest up, do something to yourself that makes you feel human and professional. For some people, it's putting on makeup, doing their hair, or applying beard oil. Putting on earrings, shoes, or even a tie (one man I know puts on a tie daily) can signal to your brain that you're in work mode.

Journal, Write, or Read: Doing some form of journaling, writing, or reading tells your brain that you're making yourself a priority and ensures you take some time to reflect, even if you get sidetracked during the day. Each morning, I write down three things I'm grateful for, what I will do to make that day great, and my mantra for the day in my Powered Path Playbook®. Some of my clients will read for a specific amount of time, a single chapter, or do some kind of devotional.

Meditation or Breathing Exercises: Starting your day with a meditation or breathing exercise (spending even as little as two minutes) can be helpful to get your mind right and ready. I often hear this practice is a resolution people can't keep, but starting your day with it ensures it gets done.

Evening Transitions

End on Time: Decide earlier in the day what time you will finish and tell your family to hold you accountable. You can do as one client did and tell yourself that your child is waiting at the bus stop, freezing in the cold weather, or getting soaked in the rain, and you need to get to the bus stop on time! This mindset helped her close down at the end of each day and actually get to her exercise class on time.

Reflect, Prioritize, and Plan: In our Powered Path Playbook®, we have space at the end of the day to reflect on our wins and what we would have done differently. We also encourage writing down at least one priority for the following day and deciding what we will do from *our* agenda in our first task block so that we can start the next day ready to go.

Meditation or Breathing Exercises: These are also great for end-of-day transitions, especially if you're in go-mode or feeling frustrated and need to get your chill on for your family. I had one remote worker client who would go to his car and sit in it for a few minutes at the end of his work day, then get out and walk in the door as if he had commuted!

Shut Down Your Computer: Instead of just shutting the lid, completely shut down your computer and put it away. Marie Noel, Senior Director of Total Rewards at Blueprint Medicines, even packs hers in her laptop bag and puts it in the closet so it's out of sight. She says, "taking a break from my screens gives me the brain space to think and tackle complex problems. I usually devise better and more creative solutions when I step away for a bit."

Transition Song: My friend Lilly Ferrick has an alarm on her phone set to play Taylor Swift's "Shake It Off" at the end of the day. My Alexa plays Robert Randolph and the Family Band "Ain't Nothing Wrong With That." It's my favorite song to dance to, and I know in those last few minutes leading up to it that I can't be working once that song starts playing! One client chose to have their Google Home tell a joke at 5:15 p.m. every day, which signaled that there would be no more work or homework for anyone in the house.

Walk Your Dog or Take a Walk: Get outside the house and away from your computer. We've been looking at screens all day, and our eyes need to look into the distance. Leave your technology at home and make it a routine, even if it's just one quick spin around the block.

TL;DR

Remote workers often work longer hours and struggle to disconnect due to blurred boundaries, constant accessibility, and pressure to be available. Without the routine of commuting and office environments, the lines between work and personal life blur further. Establishing clear start and stop transitions is crucial. Morning rituals like exercise, dressing for work, and setting a consistent start time can help. Evening routines such as defining a finish time, reflecting on the day, and fully shutting down your computer signal the end of the workday, promoting balance and prioritizing mental and physical health.

MANAGER

Dump Productivity Paranoia

Ever feel like your team is constantly on the go but never quite hitting the mark? Welcome to the world of "Productivity Paranoia." Microsoft defines it as fear from company leaders that "lost productivity is due to employees not working, even though hours worked, number of meetings, and other activity metrics have increased."[60]

There is a massive disconnect between managers who feel their employees are productive (12%) and employees who feel they are productive (87%). It boils down to managers feeling they need to *see* their team members working to believe it. I'm sure *you* need to be seen to be accountable, right (winky-winky)?[61]

This fear and disconnect can feed into overcommunication, especially between leaders and remote workers. Positive reasons could be wanting your workers to feel included and wanting to bond with them. Negative reasons include "checking in" to ensure you'll get a response back quickly, which must mean they're working, right? Yeah, they're working, *but not doing deep, focused work because otherwise, they wouldn't respond immediately.* This switchtasking leads to more mistakes and a longer time to complete tasks.

---

[60] "Hybrid Work is Just Work—Are We Doing It Wrong?," Microsoft, September 22, 2022 (https://www.microsoft.com/en-us/worklab/work-trend-index/hybrid-work-is-just-work)

[61] "Hybrid Work is Just Work—Are We Doing It Wrong?," Microsoft, September 22, 2022 (https://www.microsoft.com/en-us/worklab/work-trend-index/hybrid-work-is-just-work)

One attendee in a conference breakout session said they like to video conference with their employees at random times during the day to check in. To him, it's like stopping by someone's desk. This can feel very invasive. He thought he was being inclusive and that it was a nice gesture, but I explained that we *expected* to be interrupted in the office. I can see you walking toward my desk. You can also see my visual cues that I'm concentrating, on a call, or open to talk. Interruptions are *more disruptive* when remote because we aren't expecting them.

> "Working with RaderCo made me a better manager, which made my team happier. I learned many things that we rolled out to our whole team. I find myself paying the great ideas forward. It's not just about me." – Deb McMurray, Associate Director, Contract Operations, Biogen

This paranoia makes employees feel mistrusted, decreases morale, and causes stress. Fifty-four percent of remote workers feel like they are micromanaged. Fifty-seven percent of Gen Z employees feel they are trusted by their managers, compared to 77% of Boomers. It also causes them to focus on busy work, such as email and chats, rather than productive work.

In today's always-on work culture, it's easy for managers to fall into the trap of equating busy with productive. Unrealistic expectations pile up, and the pressure to deliver can be overwhelming. Or, our cognitive dissonance points us to that *one* worker who was lazy at home, and we attribute that characteristic to *all* remote workers. The result? Burnout, dwindling creativity, and a workforce that's disengaged and exhausted.

To avoid Productivity Paranoia, set clear, measurable outcomes and change to a Results-Oriented or Action-Oriented culture. Instead of looking at how much time team members spend on their computers or in the office, let's measure what they're getting done. Isn't it less costly and more efficient to finish the task in a shorter amount of time with fewer mistakes? If something takes six hours, why should we push it to eight? Time is arbitrary. If I'm 20% more efficient at home than in the office, why should I spend that extra time just sitting at my desk, waiting for a chat message to pop up? In-office workers often don't think about the time they spend with co-workers doing non-productive tasks, telling stories, or catching up over coffee. However, that is seen as something positive for company culture rather than a distraction or not working.

With an Outcome/Results/Action-Oriented culture, teams can focus on what truly matters. It empowers employees by letting them manage their own time and approach to tasks. It provides growth opportunities for them to find the most efficient ways to achieve goals, and they can feel even better about their contributions.

Implement tools that track outcomes, not just activity. A project management system can give you the status updates you often look for and allow you to see what each team member has done.

Use the Communications Matrix from Chapter 2 to determine the best way to contact people and keep it within their general work hours. One of my clients is a pathologist who needs a lot of deep, focused work time. But he's constantly being pinged, and if he doesn't have his chat tool open, he comes off as not being a team player or not getting back in a timely manner. What's more critical…quality work or a fast reaction?

Productivity Paranoia can profoundly impact your team and you. You can turn it off by defining success, setting realistic goals, and creating a results-oriented work environment.

TL;DR

Productivity Paranoia is the fear that employees aren't working enough despite increased activity metrics. This leads to overcommunication, micromanagement, and distrust, which causes stress and inefficiency. To combat this, shift to an outcome-oriented culture by setting clear, measurable goals, using tools that track outcomes, and respecting deep work time and communication boundaries. This approach empowers employees, improves morale, and enhances productivity.

Incorporate Virtual Team Building

As we continue to navigate remote and hybrid work setups, it's essential to acknowledge the unique challenges teams face, from communication gaps to feelings of isolation. While these obstacles are real, there are effective strategies you can implement to keep your team connected and engaged.

Problems:

Communication Gaps: Lack of face-to-face interaction can lead to misunderstandings and miscommunications. There may also be cultural or style differences that make asynchronous communication more challenging.

> I'm pretty direct in my communication and don't add a lot of "flowery" language or fluff. I tell all new team members right away, and all clients receive a link to our Email Manifesto (helloraderco.com/email-manifesto), so they know what to expect. If I don't clarify my communication style, some people may feel I'm rude or worry that I'm angry with them.

Isolation: Remote workers may feel isolated and disconnected from their team and worry that they aren't as visible or as likely to be promoted as their in-office co-workers.

Trust Issues: Building trust without physical presence can be difficult, but why would you hire someone you don't trust and then make them earn your trust? Would you sit and watch an in-office worker for a few weeks to ensure they aren't online shopping?

Solutions:

Regular Check-ins: Schedule regular video calls for team meetings and one-to-ones (but don't overdo it!). For one-to-ones, have options such as walkie-talkies so you can both get outside and talk by phone. It feels more casual, friendly, and trusting.

Virtual Team Building Activities: Organize virtual games, workshops, and social events. We've had clients who've done virtual wine tastings where everyone received a bottle, virtual campfires where they were sent the items to make s'mores at their desks, and virtual scavenger hunts. One client even had their team attend a virtual drag show!

> *"If you need help with engagement in a virtual meeting, randomly offer prizes for those who keep their video on, give feedback in the chat, and don't multitask. Prizes could include professional development books, fun coffee mugs, or small gift cards." – Helen Moses, RaderCo Vocal Communications Specialist*

Foster Inclusion: Encourage cultural awareness and inclusivity through team activities and training. Choose a cadence to spotlight a team member and allow them to talk about their heritage, family history, what they do for fun, or whatever they want to talk about. Include one question per meeting that's just fun or personal, like 1) Where is your dream vacation? 2) What's the funniest name you've had for a pet? 3) What's your favorite thing to drink during the workday? Or show us your favorite mug.

Encourage Feedback: Create channels for regular feedback to address issues promptly. You don't want to discover someone leaving because of your culture during their exit interview. Continually ask anonymously how you could do better.

Leverage Technology: Use your asynchronous tools—email, chat, screen-capture videos—and be mindful of everyone's communication overload.

Personal Touch: Celebrate milestones, birthdays, and achievements to build a sense of community. Ask people if they have any significant dates coming up or are working on something meaningful to them. When I asked this, I learned that one of our RaderCo team members was training for her first 10k, and another had been taking a Spanish class weekly and had a goal of living for one month in Mexico. This opened up conversations between teammates who spoke Spanish (and sometimes would chat in Spanish) and who ran races.

Be Flexible: Core hours make sense for many businesses, but consider a person's peak productive time. If I'm an early morning person and like to start work early and end at 3:00 p.m., respect and know that, as an adult, I can monitor my time and energy, and that's how you'll get the best out of me. Our Marketing Specialist doesn't start work until 10:00 a.m. and works later into the evening, sometimes returning at night during her creative hours. This works for me. I have access to her during core hours, but I also respect when she can be her most efficient self.

Fairness in Perks: If you have a hybrid team and you're buying lunch for the in-office staff during your meeting, send a gift certificate for a meal delivery service to your remote staff. If you have a treat in the breakroom for an in-office birthday, send a treat to your remote staff. At a minimum, if you celebrate the birthdays of in-office workers, ensure you celebrate remote workers' birthdays, too.

TL;DR

Remote and hybrid work setups have challenges like communication gaps, isolation, and trust issues. To address these, implement regular check-ins and virtual team-building activities, foster inclusion, encourage feedback, allow flexibility, and add personal touches. These strategies help keep your team connected and engaged, ensuring a cohesive and productive work environment.

C+/BUSINESS OWNER

Trust In Your Remote Workforce

In the era of remote work, trust between companies and their employees has emerged as a critical concern. Without the traditional office environment, businesses often grapple with unique challenges that can undermine this trust. Addressing these issues requires clear communication, setting expectations, effective use of technology, and fostering a culture of trust and accountability.

I've heard some real horror stories from attendees of my workshops or clients I've coached. One person stated that she was required to log in to Zoom the entire time she was clocked in. She felt smothered. I felt enraged. Do you want someone two feet away from you staring at your face all day? How can you relax? What if you scratch your nose or pull at your ear? She was so self-conscious, and this policy caused her so much stress that she quit the job.

If you can't trust your employees to work from home, they shouldn't work for you in the office either. And really, the number of work hours is arbitrary. If they can get their work done in less time, celebrate that! Don't make them continue to sit there and surf the web!

If the time of day doesn't matter, celebrate that we all have high and low points during the day of productivity and energy and allow people to capitalize on that. Don't punish a night owl by making them start work at 8:00 a.m. unless there's a real need. You may not be able to give complete flexibility, but could you have a block of four to six hours of required time, like 10:00 a.m. to 3:00 pm, and then any other work can be done when individuals are at their best? This style is best summarized by Satya Nadella, chairman and CEO of Microsoft:

> *"Our new data shows there is no one-size-fits-all approach to hybrid and remote work, as employee expectations continue to change. The only way for organizations to solve for this complexity is to embrace flexibility across their entire operating model, including the ways people work, the places they inhabit, and how they approach business process."*[62]

For some, working from home is a privilege *and* a necessity. When people need more trust in others, I wonder if *they* are untrustworthy and don't work efficiently from home and project that onto others.

---

[62] "Hybrid Work is Just Work—Are We Doing It Wrong?," Microsoft, September 22, 2022 (https://www.microsoft.com/en-us/worklab/work-trend-index/hybrid-work-is-just-work)

Did you know that most people who work from home tend to work *more hours*, not less, and are also more productive?[63]

Why?

There are fewer drive-by conversations or idle chats. We don't need to go across a building or to another floor to use the bathroom or refill our water—just a few steps. We're less likely to go out for lunch or take a break at lunch (although this behavior should be discouraged).

Remote workers feel nervous about stepping away. They're afraid if they go out for lunch (which is something familiar in a typical workplace), they may get a message during that time and "get caught" being away from their desk.

They make excuses if they can't react to your Microsoft Teams or Slack chat. They don't turn it off at night because their office is right there, and they often return to work after dinner or check email before bed.

> Please relook at your stance on trust with your remote workers. Don't create a culture of secrecy and hostility because that's what a lack of trust is. *If you can't trust them at home, you can't trust them in the office.*

---

[63] Ryan Bradshaw, "Surprising Working From Home Productivity Statistics," Apollo Technical, February 7, 2024 (https://www.apollotechnical.com/working-from-home-productivity-statistics)

Suppose you continue not to trust your employees. In that case, it could even lead to Quiet Quitting (doing the bare minimum tasks of your job description well enough that you don't get fired).[64] Consequently, this can affect your business KPIs like employee retention, attraction, bottom line, etc. To succeed at remote work, keep your employees at the center. This gives them the trust they need to give 100% to you during work time and succeed at the job.

Per an employee from Alaska, "if my company is going to come in and give me this flexibility, then I'm going to be the first to give them 100%."[65]

Per the Digital Wellness Institute eBook, 83% of employees look to their employers for guidance in navigating the pressures of remote work. Yet many employers feel ill-equipped to deal with these new pressures.[66]

Thus, there is a vast need to upskill and train to work well remotely and create a thriving remote work culture. It's also

[64] Gleb Tsipursky, PhD, "Is Remote Work Responsible for Quiet Quitting?," Forbes, December 8, 2022 (https://www.forbes.com/sites/glebtsipursky/2022/12/05/is-remote-work-responsible-for-quiet-quitting/?sh=282298da1ed5)

[65] Alex DeMarban, "Alaska Employers are Sticking With Remote Work Even Post-Pandemic," Seattle Times, October 2, 2022 (https://www.seattletimes.com/business/alaska-employers-are-sticking-with-remote-work-even-post-pandemic/)

[66] "Digital Wellness Ebook: How Purposeful Habits Improve Employee Mental Health, Retention, and Productivity," Digital Wellness Institute, (https://www.digitalwellnessinstitute.com/landing-pages/ebook-download)

one of the training topics in our Work Well Remotely series,[67] where we train managers and team members on working well *together* from home to create a culture of trust and flexibility while keeping our employees at the center of this new change and transformation.

Problems:

Lack of Visibility: Managers need their team's physical presence to gauge productivity and engagement. We're relying on face time instead of results.

Communication Gaps: Remote work can lead to misunderstandings and lack of clarity, affecting collaboration and trust.

Performance Measurement: Assessing performance and output accurately becomes a challenge without traditional supervision.

Data Security: Concerns about the security of sensitive information accessed from various locations.

Team Cohesion: Building and maintaining a strong team culture and trust is harder without face-to-face interactions.

Accountability: Ensuring remote workers are accountable for their tasks and responsibilities without direct oversight can be a managerial challenge.

---

[67] RaderCo Topics Catalog (https://www.marceyrader.com/topics-catalog)

Solutions

Clear Communication: Establish regular check-ins and a communications matrix that emphasizes which tool to use for what type of communication.

Set Expectations: Define clear goals, deadlines, and deliverables. Ensure that remote workers understand their roles and responsibilities.

Establish Core Hours: Have a four- to six-hour block where people need to be available, and then allow flexibility for them to work when they are at their best. Give people autonomy and responsibility to manage their time.

Use Technology: Leverage project management tools, collaboration platforms, and communication apps to facilitate workflow and maintain visibility (but without micromanagement).

Performance Metrics: Implement objective performance metrics and KPIs to evaluate productivity and outcomes rather than hours worked.

Data Security Measures: To protect sensitive information, invest in robust cybersecurity protocols, VPNs, and regular security training.

Build Team Cohesion: Foster team bonding through virtual team-building activities, regular video meetings, and occasional in-person meetups. Giving teams a budget to meet annually can go a long way toward making people feel connected and increasing a sense of belonging. For smaller companies, invest in an annual one- or two-day retreat where everyone comes together.

Encourage Transparency: Promote an open culture where remote workers feel comfortable sharing their progress, challenges, and ideas.

Provide Support: Offer resources for remote work setups, mental health support, and professional development opportunities.

Employee Monitoring

More than 65% of employers use monitoring software, which can erode trust among all employees. A culture of surveillance makes people feel they're under constant watch, leading to increased stress and anxiety. They are treated with suspicion instead of trust.[68] This clearly signals that management doesn't trust employees to manage their tasks without oversight. This perceived mistrust can severely damage morale, leading to disengagement and reduced motivation.

Constant monitoring can also stifle innovation and creativity. Employees who know they are being watched are less likely to take risks or think creatively.[69] It can also blur the line between

---

[68] Kayla Matthews, "Privacy vs. Productivity - How Employee Monitoring Software Backfires (and What to Use Instead)," RescueTime Blog, July 18, 2019 (https://blog.rescuetime.com/employee-monitoring-privacy-vs-productivity/)

[69] Dale Strickland, "Five Ways Transparency is Key When Monitoring Employees in the Workplace," Currentware, (https://www.currentware.com/blog/monitoring-employees-in-the-workplace-transparency/)

professional oversight and personal invasion, causing feelings of resentment and dehumanization.

When leadership monitors every action, it promotes a culture of blame where mistakes are highlighted and become targets for shame rather than being seen as opportunities for earned lessons. This results in a fear-based culture where team members are more concerned with avoiding errors (or covering them up) than achieving excellence. They will also be less likely to share their true thoughts and feelings. The psychological impact of all of it leads to disengagement and higher turnover.

While employee monitoring software can provide insights and security benefits, it is crucial to balance these with respect for employees' autonomy and privacy. Getting a general idea, summary, or anonymous report of what team members are doing is one thing; getting the exact amount of time each person is on a website, checking their email, or the number of minutes between mouse movements is another.

Microsoft Viva and the Boomerang extension report the average time before answering an email. When I see low numbers like two minutes, six minutes, etc., this isn't a sign of productivity for most roles; it's a sign that they are reactive, switchtasking, probably making more mistakes, and taking longer to complete their tasks. It's not a sign of efficiency!

Building a culture of trust requires transparency, open communication, and a genuine belief in the team's ability to perform without constant oversight.

TL;DR

Trust is vital in remote work, but companies face challenges like lack of visibility, communication gaps, and accountability issues. Trust should focus on outcomes, not hours, and embrace flexible schedules and performance metrics. Over-monitoring erodes trust and stifles innovation. Balancing oversight with respect for employees' autonomy is crucial for a productive and motivated remote workforce.

Cultivate a Culture of Inclusion

Cultivating an inclusive culture for your remote and hybrid teams doesn't have to be rocket science. Think of it like hosting a virtual party where everyone feels welcome and heard, no matter where they're tuning in from. Ready to turn your team into a cohesive, happy crew? Let's dive into the problems and then solutions that are fun and effective ways to make sure every voice counts and every team member feels like a star, whether they're working from home or the office.

Problems:

Communication Gaps: Remote and hybrid team members may feel left out due to missed information or a lack of engagement.

Unequal Access to Resources: Remote employees might not have the same access to tools and resources as in-office staff.

Isolation and Disconnection: Remote workers may feel isolated and disconnected from the team.

Meeting Fatigue: Virtual meetings can be exhausting and may only accommodate some time zones.

Lack of Cultural Awareness: Team members might feel misunderstood or undervalued.

Feedback Challenges: Remote workers may find giving and receiving feedback harder due to a lack of non-verbal cues and fewer casual interactions.

Recognition Disparities: Remote employees might feel their achievements go unnoticed.

Policy Inconsistencies: Inconsistent policies can lead to feelings of unfair treatment.

Leadership Disconnect: Leaders may be disconnected from remote team members' needs.

Company Perks: Many perks, such as fitness centers and Happy Hours, are only available in the office, making remote employees feel disconnected.

Solutions:

Communication Channels: Implement clear and consistent communication channels and create your matrix so everyone knows which one is for what circumstance. Hold regular virtual meetings (but not too many; we're overloaded!) to ensure everyone is in the loop.

Access: Provide necessary equipment, software, and support to all employees, regardless of location. Consider stipends for home office setups beyond the typical desk and chair. What about a screen backdrop, high-quality webcam, or headphones? You're saving money on commercial real estate, right?

Virtual Social Interactions: Host online team-building activities, coffee chats, and virtual happy hours (but don't make them mandatory if they are after work hours). Send gift cards for meal-delivery services, coffee shops, or a treat box to make s'mores.

Thoughtful Meetings: Schedule meetings thoughtfully, rotate meeting times to accommodate different time zones, and encourage asynchronous communication, such as video screen capture, where possible.

Cultural Awareness: Promote cultural awareness through training programs, celebrate diverse holidays, and encourage sharing of cultural experiences.

Feedback: Implement regular, anonymous feedback mechanisms and create a culture of open communication and continuous improvement. Maintain regular one-to-one check-ins and encourage time to connect on a personal level.

Achievement Recognition: Ensure recognition programs are inclusive and celebrate achievements publicly across all team members.

Standardized HR Policies: Policies need to be flexible and inclusive, offering all employees benefits like mental health days and flexible work hours. If a mental health counselor is onsite, remote workers should also have access to a remote counselor.

Leadership Connection: Offer opportunities for them to get to know leadership with quarterly Ask Me Anything or virtual coffee sessions.

Remote Perks: Create a program to give remote employees perks like a meal delivery service gift card or discount or reimbursement for a gym membership or fitness class. You can also ask *them* what perks would be best and let them choose from a buffet of items. I like the website Loop & Tie which allows recipients to pick out their own gift within a certain budget range.

By addressing these problems with thoughtful solutions, companies can create an inclusive and thriving culture for their remote and hybrid teams. This will make every team member feel like a superstar, whether in the office or at home.

TL;DR

Cultivating an inclusive culture for remote and hybrid teams is like hosting a virtual party where everyone feels welcome. Address issues like communication gaps, resource inequality, isolation, meeting fatigue, cultural awareness, feedback challenges, recognition disparities, policy inconsistencies, and unequal perks. Solutions include clear communication, providing resources, fostering virtual social interactions, thoughtful meeting scheduling, promoting cultural awareness, regular feedback, inclusive recognition, flexible HR policies, leadership connections, and remote perks. These steps ensure every team member feels valued in the office or home.

References

Nicholas Bloom, "How working from home works out," Stanford Institute for Economic Policy Research, June 2020 (https://siepr.stanford.edu/publications/policy-brief/how-working-home-works-out)

Ryan Bradshaw, "Surprising Working From Home Productivity Statistics," Apollo Technical, February 7, 2024 (https://www.apollotechnical.com/working-from-home-productivity-statistics)

Alex DeMarban, "Alaska Employers are Sticking With Remote Work Even Post-Pandemic," Seattle Times, October 2, 2022 (https://www.seattletimes.com/business/alaska-employers-are-sticking-with-remote-work-even-post-pandemic/)

Margaret Faso, "Study Finds Fully Remote Work Leads to Fewer Promotions," HR Policy Association, January 19, 2024 (https://www.hrpolicy.org/insight-and-research/resources/2024/hr_workforce/public/01/study-finds-fully-remote-work-leads-to-fewer-promo)

Kayla Matthews, "Privacy vs. Productivity - How Employee Monitoring Software Backfires (and What to Use Instead)," RescueTime Blog, July 18, 2019 (https://blog.rescuetime.com/employee-monitoring-privacy-vs-productivity/)

Luciana Paulise, "The 2022 Status of Remote Work and Top Future Predictions," Forbes, December 8, 2022 (https://www.forbes.com/sites/lucianapaulise/2022/12/08/the-2022-status-of-remote-work-and-top-future-predictions/)

Marcey Rader, "Why snackable Moments are Your New Productivity Hack," RaderCo https://www.helloraderco.com/snackable-moments/

Ryan Ray M. Reyes, "Hybrid Work: From 'new' to 'now' normal," PWC, July 4, 2024 (https://www.pwc.com/ph/en/tax/tax-publications/taxwise-or-otherwise/2024/hybrid-work-from-new-to-now-normal.html)

Dale Strickland, "Five Ways Transparency is Key When Monitoring Employees in the Workplace," Currentware, (https://www.currentware.com/blog/monitoring-employees-in-the-workplace-transparency/)

Gleb Tsipursky, PhD, "Is Remote Work Responsible for Quiet Quitting?," Forbes, December 8, 2022 (https://www.forbes.com/sites/glebtsipursky/2022/12/05/is-remote-work-responsible-for-quiet-quitting/?sh=282298da1ed5)

Gleb Tsipursky, PhD, "The Surprising Truth About Remote Work Productivity," Psychology Today, April 4, 2023 (https://www.psychologytoday.com/intl/blog/intentional-insights/202303/the-surprising-truth-about-remote-work-productivity)

"Digital Wellness Ebook: How Purposeful Habits Improve Employee Mental Health, Retention, and Productivity," Digital Wellness Institute, (https://www.digitalwellnessinstitute.com/landing-pages/ebook-download)

"Hybrid Work is Just Work—Are We Doing It Wrong?," Microsoft, September 22, 2022 (https://www.microsoft.com/en-us/worklab/work-trend-index/hybrid-work-is-just-work)

"Remote, controlled—This changes everything: Five key actions companies can take now to operationalize their remote work program," Deloitte, December 12, 2022 (https://www.deloitte.com/global/en/about/press-room/deloitte-remote-controlled.html)

CHAPTER 6

VACATION AND TIME OFF

Taking a vacation is not just a luxury; it's necessary to maintain optimal mental and physical health. And believe it or not, it also increases our productivity. Stepping away from work allows for rest and the opportunity to gain fresh perspectives. Yet, many companies fail to encourage this practice effectively. According to a study conducted by ELVTR of 2,300 workers over 18 years old, a staggering 68% of people work on vacation across all demographics.[70] Flip that number, and you'll see that only *32% manage to disconnect entirely.*

Reasons for Working on Vacation

- **Need for Control**: 15% of people say they work because they need to be in control. What are you sacrificing for this? Are you disempowering your team or the people who cover for you due to micromanaging?

---

[70] "America's Alarming (Lack of) Work-Life Balance," ELVTR, (https://elvtr.com/blog/americas-alarming-lack-of-work-life-balance)

- **Love for the Job:** 27% work because they adore their job and don't mind working on vacation. But does their family feel the same? I love what I do, but I also know that it takes time away from my family and doesn't allow me to truly rest.

- **No One to Delegate To:** 37% of individuals don't have anyone to whom they can offload their tasks.

Anticipatory Stress

When workers have trouble disconnecting from work, it can impact their mental health. Anticipatory stress is people's anxiety or nervousness about an upcoming event, such as a vacation. Worrying about potential issues that might come up can significantly impact both the employee and their family. Constantly thinking about what could go wrong can lead to mental exhaustion before the vacation even starts!

> *"My husband always says, 'You're never more stressed than the week before you go on vacation.'"* – *Emily Crookston, Owner of The Pocket PhD*

During vacation, the worry can lead to lost sleep and the inability to truly relax. Our families feel it, too. One person's stress can affect the whole family. That little argument or misunderstanding may have nothing to do with the price of the ice cream but is more about you thinking about your work piling up or missing something important. You can't be in the moment, and you've now spent time thinking about work instead of enjoying the beach or mountains. Is it worth your family time? Or if money talks, is it worth the $10,000 you spent on that cruise?

TL;DR

Regular vacations and time off are necessary to avoid burnout and ensure that workers maintain optimal mental and physical health. However, only 32% of American workers manage to disconnect when they're on vacation. This includes the need for control, love of the job, and no one to delegate responsibilities to.

Problems:

Creating a Culture of Guilt: Employees often feel guilty for taking time off, fearing they'll be seen as less dedicated. A 2023 Pew survey of 5,188 workers showed that 49% are afraid to take a vacation because they'll fall too far behind at work, and 19% feel it will hurt their chance for promotion.[71]

Lack of Encouragement: Companies that don't actively promote vacations miss the chance to boost employee morale and productivity. In the ELVTR study, 35% feel the need to work on vacation, and 18% are asked to work by their *managers*.[72]

Poor Coverage Plans: Ineffective vacation coverage leads to stress for the vacationing employee and their colleagues.

---

[71] Juliana Menasce Horowitz and Kim Parker, "How Americans View Their Jobs," Pew Research Center, March 30, 2023 (https://www.pewresearch.org/social-trends/2023/03/30/how-americans-view-their-jobs/)

[72] "America's Alarming (Lack of) Work-Life Balance," ELVTR, (https://elvtr.com/blog/americas-alarming-lack-of-work-life-balance)

Overloaded Workload on Return: Returning to an insurmountable pile of work can negate the benefits of the vacation itself and make people feel like they have to check email on vacation.

Solutions:

Lead by Example: Leadership should actively take and promote vacations. When executives and managers take time off, it signals to employees that it's acceptable and encouraged.

Vacation Policies: Implement clear, supportive policies emphasizing the importance of taking time off. Policies should be easy to understand and apply without excessive red tape.

Turn off access: Turning off email access relieves the vacationer from the impulse to check. Some companies even auto-delete messages and use an autoresponder to alert the sender.

> *"True magic happens when you fully unplug during a vacation. Far too often, employees steal glances at their emails even on paid time off, preventing their minds and bodies from gaining the true mental and physical benefits of rest. Taking a break from the constant stream of information and daily stimulation allows for deeper clarity and a greater appreciation of the world around you." – Amanda Chay, RaderCo Stress Management and Mindfulness Specialist*

No-Guilt Environment: Foster a culture where vacation is seen as a right, not a privilege. Ensure that employees feel no guilt or fear of reprisal when requesting time off.

Encourage Regular Breaks: Promote regular breaks throughout the year, not just a single annual vacation. Short, frequent breaks can be just as beneficial. Make sure that employees use all of their vacation time.

Comprehensive Coverage Plans: Develop effective coverage plans to manage workloads while employees are on vacation. Ensure that no single person is overwhelmed by covering for multiple colleagues. Assign a gatekeeper when people are out so only that person can contact the vacationing team member.

Flexible Scheduling: Offer flexibility in scheduling vacations to accommodate different employee needs and personal circumstances.

Post-Vacation Support: Help employees transition back smoothly by allowing them to work offline on their first day back.

Celebrate Time Off: Recognize and celebrate employees' vacations and time off in company communications. Highlight the benefits of vacations in newsletters or meetings. Give an incentive like gift cards for them to spend *only on vacation*.

Regular Reminders: Send regular reminders about the importance of taking time off. Use internal communications to share stories of how vacations have positively impacted employees' well-being and productivity.

Anonymous Feedback: Allow employees to provide anonymous feedback on vacation policies and culture. Use this feedback to make continuous improvements.

Temporary Staffing: For someone on parental leave, short-term disability, or some other kind of extensive leave, consider temporary staffing to relieve the rest of the team.

Levels

Action steps for Individuals:
- Set No-Meeting Days
- Alert Stakeholders
- Work Offline or Paused

Action steps for Managers:
- Model Good Behavior
- Assign a Gatekeeper and Delegate
- Document Bottlenecks

Action steps for C+/Business Owners:
- Promote a Positive Vacation Culture
- Consider Company Shutdowns

INDIVIDUAL

Set No-Meeting Days

Before you set sail, block your calendar *the day before you leave and your first day back.* This isn't just about avoiding meetings but giving yourself VIP time to wrap up loose ends and ease back into work. Whether your vacation is six months out or next week, block those dates *now.* It will guard you against last-minute scheduling chaos.

TL;DR

Don't schedule any meetings the day before you leave and the day you return.

Alert Stakeholders

Update your email signature two to three weeks before your vacation to announce your out-of-office dates. Use a standout color—like red or purple—and make it eye-catching. For instance, *"Heads up! I'll be out of the office and out of the inbox from May 15 to May 23."* This alerts colleagues and clients early on and reduces last-minute scrambles.

About a week before you leave, email the key people you work with, stakeholders, and top clients, alerting them that you will be out of the office. Ask them to request anything they need from you or, if you are waiting on something from them, to be delivered 48 hours before you leave. This way, you have a day to turn it around and aren't left scrambling on your last day when someone realizes you'll be out of the office and has a last-minute request.

Example: I'll be out of the office on an unplugged vacation with my family from July 16 to July 26 for my daughter's first trip to Disney. Because all my attention will be spent on her, I won't check my email, texts, or phone. Please reply with anything you need from me by COB on July 13 so I can turn it around for you and not leave you hanging while I'm out.

Your out-of-office message should be clear that you will *not* check email since many people often do. Let them know exactly who to contact and for what reason. In my autoresponder, I make it fun and tell people where I'll be and what I'll do. People love to read it, and I often get even more fun responses. Then, I provide links to things they may request from me, like a meeting to discuss an upcoming training, a coaching session, or my media kit. Think about the common questions you're asked. Can you record a short Loom video or provide a link to an FAQ? Can you include the contact information for your backup for anything urgent?

Below is an example out-of-office message. When I send it, I include embedded links, indicated by the underline.

I'm at my favorite cottage in Pittsboro, editing my next book on Health-Powered Productivity for individual contributors, managers, and C+/business owners. I've had my HungryRoot box delivered and am hunkering down until Sunday.

*Wanna know what 50 challenges I took on before my 50th birthday? Check out **our latest podcast episode.***

In the meantime…

*Check out my brand-spankin' new **Speaker Reel**!*

*Do you have **The Relentless Pursuit of More?***

*Need a speaker for your conference or team training? Schedule a **Speaker Connection Call**.*

*Need personal coaching to guide you in creating time guardrails, improving your focus and attention, and implementing healthy habits? Schedule a **Discovery Call.***

*Only have 3-15 minutes to gather bite-sized productivity nuggets? Check out our **podcast episodes**.*

Extremely unusual productivity emergency? Call me directly at XXX-XXX-XXXX.

Feel free to have fun with your email autoresponder while providing your recipients with any necessary information. This playful approach will make them want to read it and may even make them feel more connected to you. Jason Deshayes, CEO of Cook Wealth, has said that his auto-response messages enhance client relationships because they learn about him and often want to hear about his trip when he returns.

Here's a sample of one of his messages:

As a family tradition, my wife takes each of our kids on a "10-Year-Old" trip. She's off to Universal Studios with our son, Levi, having a blast at the pool and the Wizarding World of Harry Potter. My other two kids and I are hanging out for the week. While I'll check email and phone messages periodically, I'd love to help you avoid service delays. Here are some great contact points to help you out:

If you're a "self-service" type of person, you can book time on my calendar on my Calendly page [CALENDLY LINK].

If you have a specific tax need, email our team at XXXX@ cookwealth.com.

Administrative questions, such as "Can I get a copy of my return?," "I need to get funds transferred in/out of my account," or "Can I schedule a meeting with Jason?" are great for Adam Miles (XXXX@cookwealth.com). If you haven't had a chance to interact with Adam yet (he's new to our team), you should. He's a stellar guy.

Elliot Williams (XXXX@cookwealth.com) and Jake Rudy (XXXX@cookwealth.com) will handle planning items while I'm out. They are also amazing new members of our team.

If you have an immediate need but are unsure who to contact, please call the office at 919.XXX.XXXX, and our fantastic team will find the right person to help you.

I look forward to reconnecting with you when I return to the office on August 21st!

TL;DR

Update your email signature with out-of-office dates two to three weeks before your vacation using standout colors to alert colleagues and clients. A week before leaving, email key contacts to request needed actions or follow-ups 48 hours before departure to avoid last-minute rushes. Clearly state in your autoresponder that you won't be checking email, provide alternative contacts, and include fun details about your trip.

Work Offline or Paused

Keep your out-of-office (OOO) on for one day longer than you will be gone. For example, if you return on July 16th, put your OOO on through July 17. On your first day back, you can catch up on all your emails and tasks while you were out without people pinging you with new stuff or having a conversation.

Working offline in Outlook or pausing your inbox in Gmail can be a game-changer on your first day back. You already know how to do this from Chapter 1 on Focus and Attention. After vacation, put it into action starting your workday by downloading all your emails in Outlook or unpausing all of them in Gmail. Then, click *Work Offline* or *Pause* and process your email without new emails coming in or starting conversations. Once people know you're back, the floodgates are open! When you're all caught up, toggle back to the online mode to send all responses in one go.

I've seen people catch up within a couple of hours, rather than a couple of weeks, by simply taking this first day to work offline. It also helps to avoid the pre-return peek, where people feel compelled to check their email the night before they return to work because they know the onslaught will occur as soon as they begin.

Bonus tip: Remove the email and chat app from your phone while you're away. The extra steps of downloading and logging in again may cause just enough friction to keep you from doing it.

"Your email tricks were AWESOME! After a two-week vacation, I spent less time catching up on email than I normally do after two days out of the office!" – Anne Mayer, Associate Director, Speciality Operations, Biogen

TL;DR

Extend your out-of-office by one day beyond your return date to catch up on emails without new interruptions. Use *Work Offline* in Outlook or *Inbox Pause* in Gmail to manage messages and avoid new conversations while you catch up.

MANAGER

Model Good Behavior

You set the tone for how people take vacations at your company. If you tell your team to take a vacation and you end up carrying over three weeks into the new year (or what's worse, lose those days) or tell them they don't have to check their email but then respond to their messages while on your cruise to the Bahamas, you've destroyed trust. Also, your actions tell them that, while you say you don't want them to work, you actually expect them to. *Didn't it drive you bonkers when your parents said, "do as I say, not as I do?"* Working while you're on "vacation" can also be disempowering to them. They may perceive it as a lack of trust—you don't feel they can handle things while you are away. They can't hold down the fort. It doesn't matter what you say; if you are in a position of authority, and you are because you're a manager, your actions will stick, and if you email on vacation, they will feel compelled to do so as well. They may feel obliged to keep up on the sly even if you don't see it. To shift this behavior, take your vacation and promote positive experiences when you return. Empower your team to figure it out and do their job while you're out.

"I'm back to dancing! I used to work so much that I stopped going out for live music and hikes with my dog. Now, I'm more present with my sweetheart and have scheduled three vacations in the next six months. Thanks to your tips, I'm enjoying life again!"
– Janet Boudreau, Vistage Chair

TL;DR

As a manager, your actions set the vacation culture. If you urge vacations but don't take them yourself or respond to work emails while you're away, you undermine trust and suggest you expect your team to work during their time off. Take your time off, fully disconnect, and empower your team to take over while you're away.

Assign a Gatekeeper and Delegate

For those managers who really need to be available during mission-critical times, such as a product launch, waiting for FDA approval, or with a smaller or newer team, assign one gatekeeper or sentry. This person relentlessly guards your vacation from people so you can recharge your batteries. *Only the gatekeeper can contact you.* Everyone else needs to go through them. Tell the gatekeeper to contact you via phone or text, not your work email (because then you'll see all the other emails). Also, clearly define what constitutes a true emergency and what can be left until you return.

This gatekeeper may be an assistant but could also be one of your team members who you have delegated as your backup, stand-in, or deputy. Fully brief your backup with the necessary information, program access, and decision-making powers.

Equip them well so they can handle anything in your absence. Our Client Concierge and Marketing Specialist, Lisa, is my deputy when I'm on vacation.

She processes some of my emails, archiving any that I don't need to see, like notifications or marketing messages; provides answers or gives people items like program flyers, headshots, or bios; and leaves the items I need to address in the inbox. We use Voxer as our messaging app for work; if something she needs is urgent, she can Voxer me. This means I'm not going into my inbox, and since it's asynchronous, I can read/listen and respond when convenient. She will even copy and paste or screenshot an email and put it into Voxer to keep me out of my inbox (because it's too hard not to peek at other things when I'm in there). Before I leave, I ensure she has access to essential tools like our course platform and marketing tool for a smooth handover.

Empowering her to manage for me when I'm gone is a highlight of the quarter for her. When we do our reflections, it is always a Big Win or What Worked Well. She feels good about what she has accomplished and is always excited about how much she can keep me unplugged. It also allows us to see any bottlenecks and change a process when we find minor things that are broken or can be streamlined.

Lastly, tell your team *not* to copy you on all the emails while you're away. Otherwise, you'll be bombarded by an inbox full of emails you don't need. Tell them you trust them to give you a report or update when you return.

"Thank you, thank you, thank you! I took a two-week vacation (I had never done that before!) and was able to fully disconnect. The first few days back to work after any vacation have typically been stressful and involve late nights on my laptop. I left on time every day and didn't work at night at all. SUCCESS!!!!!!!" – Andrea Pereira, Senior HR Business Partner

TL;DR

For mission-critical times when you must be available, assign a gatekeeper to guard your vacation. This person filters all communications, contacting you only for true emergencies via phone or text to avoid your work email. The gatekeeper, who could be an assistant or team member, should be well-briefed, have access to necessary tools, and possess decision-making power. This ensures you can recharge while they manage in your absence.

Document Bottlenecks

Want to make the next vacation even smoother? Ask your team to document bottlenecks when someone, including you, is gone. Any snags they ran into, questions they couldn't answer, or programs they couldn't access go into a shared document. It's not to point fingers or blame; it's simply to improve the process for the next person.

At your next meeting, ask your team member who took a vacation to share something positive about their vacation upon returning, like they spent time with their grandkids, read four books, got a lot of rest, or felt more relaxed. Ask what could have been better when preparing or when they returned. Then, ask the team if there is anything 1) they could have done to make the process more streamlined and 2) the vacationer could have done (maybe they missed giving access to something). Create a culture where calling out bottlenecks is celebrated and encouraged so that it doesn't continue to happen.

Do the same process when you are gone and create a culture in which your team members are fearless in holding you accountable for seamless time off (and not checking in!).

TL;DR

To make vacations smoother, have your team document any bottlenecks encountered during absences in a shared document. Discuss positive vacation experiences and possible improvements in team meetings, and encourage a culture that celebrates identifying and resolving bottlenecks.

C+/BUSINESS OWNER

Promote a Positive Vacation Culture

Executives are crucial in ensuring employees take time off by modeling good behavior. Having real, unplugged time off is even more important for Millennials and Gen Z, but they are often the most afraid to take it. These generations place a higher value on unplugged time off because having grown up with the internet and smartphones, they know the toll screentime takes on mental health. They also are more focused on work-life balance and self-care and don't place the same stigma on mental health as Gen X and Boomers. Half of employees said they get nervous when asking for time off (this increases to 61% for Millennials), and 76% wish their employer encouraged it more.[73]

Things to consider:

- Don't allow employees to carry too much vacation into the following year. We need people to take breaks to recharge for their mental health and overall well-being and to feel more engaged at work.
- Discourage emails while people are out.
- Normalize time off and recognize people who take vacation days. In your company newsletter, spotlight someone who recently vacationed.
- Regularly audit vacation usage across the organization. Are there specific roles or teams that aren't taking them as they should?

Creative vacation policies

Airbnb - Offers employees an annual stipend to travel and stay in Airbnb listings worldwide, promoting the company's product and encouraging a global perspective.

---

[73] Shalene Gupta, "Your Employees Are Afraid to Take PTO, But Half Are Playing Hooky Anyway," Fast Company, May 21, 2014 (https://www.fastcompany.com/91128407/employees-play-hooky-work-pto-fear-survey)

Salesforce - Provides a wellness reimbursement program that includes vacation expenses, allowing employees to take time off for personal wellness activities.

FullContact - Offers employees $7,500 to go on vacation, with the condition that they completely disconnect from work during their time off. Now *that* is going all in!

Asana - Offers employees a paid six-week sabbatical every four years to pursue personal projects or passions.

The Huffington Post - Gives employees the option to auto-delete or auto-file all emails while on vacation. If you send a message, you'll get a response saying that person is out of the office, and your message will be deleted.[74]

Unlimited Vacation

It sounds like a dream, but it isn't always what it's cracked up to be.

Pros:

Employee Attraction and Retention: Unlimited vacation can be a strong recruitment tool, attracting top talent by signaling

---

[74] Caroline Gregoire, "HuffPost's New Tool Will Automatically Delete Emails for Vacationing Employees," Huffington Post, July 31, 2015 (https://www.huffpost.com/entry/huffpost-email-deletion-tool-vaca tion_n_55ba97a8e4b0b23e3ce21f5f)

trust and flexibility.[75] Employees report higher job satisfaction and morale because they feel trusted and valued.

Operational Benefits: It simplifies HR processes by eliminating the need to track vacation days and reduces the burden of managing unused leave payouts when employees depart.[76] It can also save money on the financial payouts of accrued vacation days.

Health and Productivity: Employees take necessary breaks and are more likely to take time off when they're sick, which can reduce burnout.

Cons:

Underutilization: Employees may take *less* time off due to uncertainty about what is acceptable, leading to decreased overall vacation usage and potential burnout.[77] Without clear guidelines, employees might feel pressured to minimize their time off to demonstrate dedication, undermining the policy's intent.

Management Challenges: Without a fixed number of vacation days, difficulties can arise in planning and managing team schedules, especially during peak times. If some employees

[75] "Unlimited PTO (Paid Time Off): Pros and Cons," Oggi Talent, February 6, 2024 (https://oggitalent.com/unlimited-pto-paid-time-off-pros-and-cons/)

[76] Dane Hurtubise, "The Pros and Cons of Unlimited Time Off," Employee Benefit News, February 3, 2015 (https://www.benefitnews.com/news/the-pros-and-cons-of-unlimited-pto)

[77] "Unlimited Vacation: Is it Too Good to Be True?," ClickTime, (https://www.clicktime.com/blog/unlimited-vacation-policy-pros-and-cons)

take more time off than others, this can lead to perceptions of favoritism or resentment.[78]

Not One-Size-Fits-All: This policy may not work for some organizations, especially those with hourly or seasonal workers, i.e., retail, manufacturing, hospitality, or healthcare.[79]

TL;DR

Executives, like managers, must model good vacation behavior and encourage unplugged time off. Prevent excessive vacation carryover, discourage work emails during time off, and recognize employees who take breaks to boost well-being and engagement. While unlimited vacation attracts talent and simplifies HR, it can lead to underuse and management challenges if not well-implemented and may not suit all organizational types.

Company Shut-Downs

Company shutdowns, where the entire organization takes time off simultaneously, offer several significant benefits. While not *all* types of companies can do this, you may want to consider some version of this for adoption. For example, you may have to operate with a skeleton crew (provide some other type of

---

[78] Dane Hurtubise, "The Pros and Cons of Unlimited Time Off," Employee Benefit News, February 3, 2015 (https://www.benefitnews.com/news/the-pros-and-cons-of-unlimited-pto)

[79] "Unlimited Vacation: Is it Too Good to Be True?," ClickTime, (https://www.clicktime.com/blog/unlimited-vacation-policy-pros-and-cons)

incentive for these folks) or get creative, but there are definitely a lot of pros to doing it.

Complete Disconnect: Employees can fully disconnect without worrying about work piling up, feeling FOMO, or missing essential communications. Everyone's batteries are recharged and ready to go!

Reduced Burnout: Regular shutdowns help prevent burnout by ensuring *everyone* gets substantial downtime.

Equal Breaks: Since everyone takes a break simultaneously, there's no disparity in workloads or guilt for taking time off.

Shared Experiences: Company shutdowns can be coupled with team-building activities or retreats, strengthening team bonds.

Predictable Schedules: Planned shutdowns allow for better planning and resource management.

Maintenance Opportunities: It's a perfect time for system upgrades or maintenance without disrupting daily operations. Yes, people are working and have to perform these upgrades, so provide them with something special, like an airline or hotel gift certificate, and then ensure they take time off.

Care Outside of Work: This demonstrates the company's commitment to caring about its employees' well-being, families, and personal commitments.

Incorporating company shutdowns can be a strategic move to boost overall organizational health, productivity, and morale.

One RaderCo client, Blueprint Medicines, has two global shutdowns yearly, which they call wellness weeks, one the week of July 4th and one the week between Christmas and New Year's Day. Every person we've ever coached states what a benefit it is. Even if they choose not to go on vacation that week, they can do things at home or with their family and not feel like they have a mountain of work to catch up on. It allows employees the time and space to recharge mentally and physically so they can return revitalized and ready to advance on the company's scientific goals and business growth.

> "I love that we have two company shutdowns each year, especially the one in the summer. Since everyone is out of the office at the same time, I can really take time off, disconnect, and relax with my family because nothing is accumulating while I'm gone."
> – Aixa Rivera, Senior Director, Human Resources Business Partner, Blueprint Medicines

Another RaderCo biotech client, Vertex Pharmaceuticals, shuts down for one week in August and December, giving its employees the time to relax without worrying about missing meetings or accumulating emails.

Examples of companies with time off

Etsy - Has "Together Week" and shuts down operations annually, simultaneously giving all employees time off to ensure true downtime without work piling up.

Adobe - Closes the entire company for one week twice a year, during the summer and winter, ensuring all employees get a break without work stress.

Video Narrative - A video production company based in Portland, Oregon (and creator of my speaking reel, marceyrader.com/reel), closes its office for one week each in the spring, summer, and during Thanksgiving week, as well as the week of Christmas, through the end of the year. They feel their team is more productive after each break. They let their clients know about the break about two to three weeks before they shut down. When I was their client, I received one of these messages and gave a virtual high five! They also focus on mission-critical tasks leading up to the breaks so that they can really be off when the week arrives. The founder, Chris West, doesn't email employees during the break and requests that they don't email him either.

> *"Taking this amount of time off each year has never affected our sales. It's the opposite. And it has resulted in us having virtually no turnover in over ten years."*
> *– Chris West, Founder of Video Narrative*

Baldwin& - The first Certified B-Corp creative agency, offers fun company-wide days off for its team members. In addition to unlimited PTO, the agency recognizes *at least one* monthly holiday.

- January – New Year's Day
- January – MLK Day
- February – Super Bowl Monday (because they know anyone who watches it won't be productive the next day, so why not?)

- February – Presidents Day
- March – March Madness Friday (they're in North Carolina, y'all)
- April – Good Friday
- May – Memorial Day
- June – Juneteenth
- July – Independence Day
- August – Too Hot To Work Day (they made this one up)
- September – Labor Day
- October – Indigenous Peoples Day
- November – Veterans Day
- November – Thanksgiving
- December – Holiday Break (the week between Christmas and New Year)

Can you think of other holidays? If you have a company with families, what about giving them Halloween off? You could block off back-to-school days, where even if someone doesn't have kids, it's still fun to have the day off in August and get nostalgic about buying new clothes and a new backpack. You could also consider Summer Hours, where you end at noon or go all in and shut down on Fridays throughout the summer.

TL;DR

Company shutdowns, where everyone takes time off simultaneously, offer full disconnection, reduced burnout, and equal breaks for all, enhancing productivity and morale. These planned shutdowns also allow for better scheduling and maintenance. While creative solutions or skeleton crews may be needed, the benefits make it worthwhile.

References

Caroline Gregoire, "HuffPost's New Tool Will Automatically Delete Emails for Vacationing Employees," Huffington Post, July 31, 2015 (https://www. huffpost.com/entry/huffpost-email-deletion-tool-vac ation_n_55ba97a8e4b0b23e3ce21f5f)

Shalene Gupta, "Your Employees Are Afraid to Take PTO, But Half Are Playing Hooky Anyway," Fast Company, May 21, 2014 (https://www.fastcompany.com/91128407/ employees-play-hooky-work-pto-fear-survey)

Dane Hurtubise, "The Pros and Cons of Unlimited Time Off," Employee Benefit News, February 3, 2015 (https://www.benefitnews.com/news/ the-pros-and-cons-of-unlimited-pto)

Juliana Menasce Horowitz and Kim Parker, "How Americans View Their Jobs," Pew Research Center, March 30, 2023 (https://www.pewresearch.org/social-trends/2023/03/30/ how-americans-view-their-jobs/)

"America's Alarming (Lack of) Work-Life Balance," ELVTR, (https://elvtr.com/blog/ americas-alarming-lack-of-work-life-balance)

"Unlimited PTO (Paid Time Off): Pros and Cons," Oggi Talent, February 6, 2024 (https://oggitalent.com/ unlimited-pto-paid-time-off-pros-and-cons/)

"Unlimited Vacation: Is it Too Good to Be True?," ClickTime, (https://www.clicktime.com/blog/ unlimited-vacation-policy-pros-and-cons)

CHAPTER 7

HEALTHY HABITS

Ever noticed how a plant perks up with a bit of sunlight and water? Guess what? We're not all that different. We spend a considerable chunk of our lives at work, so why not make it a place where we can grow? Where we don't lie dormant or, worse, wither away and die? This chapter dives into the magic of promoting healthy behaviors at work and why it's the secret sauce for a happier, more productive team.

Imagine this: You walk into the office (or log into your virtual workspace), and everyone is energized, focused, and even cracking a few smiles. No, it's not a utopian dream. It's what happens when companies prioritize health and why RaderCo focuses on Health-Powered Productivity™. We're talking about everything from encouraging midday stretch breaks to creating spaces where creativity and relaxation can bloom.

But it's not just about feeling good—there are serious perks for businesses, too.[80] Healthier employees mean fewer sick days, higher engagement, and even better bottom lines (and maybe stronger bottoms if we move more!). Plus, who wouldn't want to work in a place that feels more like a supportive community than a stress factory?

So, grab your water bottle, stretch out those typing fingers, and get ready to explore how fostering a healthy workplace culture can help you reclaim your workday and transform your 9-to-5 grind into a place where everyone can shine.

TL;DR

Promoting healthy behaviors can transform our workplaces into environments where everyone can flourish. This chapter explores the benefits of Health-Powered Productivity™, from reducing aches and pains to boosting mental well-being and engagement. Healthier employees mean fewer sick days, higher productivity, and lower healthcare costs. Solutions include ergonomic workstations, regular breaks, mental health support, and physical activity programs. It's about turning the 9-to-5 grind into a place where everyone shines.

---

[80] Kara Dennison, "Why companies should prioritize employee health and happiness in 2024," Forbes, October 24, 2023 (https://www.forbes.com/sites/karadennison/2023/10/24/why-companies-should-prioritize-employee-health-and-happiness-in-2024/)

Problems:

Aches and Pains: Poor posture and prolonged sitting can lead to back pain, neck strain, and repetitive strain injuries (RSIs).

Sedentary Lifestyles: A desk job can contribute to health problems like diabetes and heart disease. Remote workers may especially feel this because they fear stepping away from their desks.

Eye Strain: Prolonged screen time can cause digital eye strain, leading to headaches and blurred vision.

Stress and Burnout: High workloads, tight deadlines, job insecurity, and constant connectivity can lead to chronic stress and burnout.

Anxiety and Depression: Isolation and lack of social interaction in remote or desk-based work can contribute to mental health issues.

Cognitive Fatigue: Continuous multitasking and digital distractions reduce focus and cognitive performance.

Decreased Productivity: Health issues lead to lower productivity and increased absenteeism.

Higher Healthcare Costs: Companies bear higher healthcare costs due to employee health problems.

Reduced Employee Engagement: Poor health and well-being can decrease employee engagement and morale.

Solutions:

Ergonomic Workstations: Invest in adjustable chairs and sit-stand desks. It's a bonus if you offer a few treadmills and bike desks for people to use in the office.

Regular Breaks: Encourage regular breaks, screen-free lunches, and stretching exercises.

Walking Meetings: Encourage a culture of walking meetings to increase creativity and productivity and break free from the caves made up of four walls.

Mental Health Support: Provide access to mental health resources through an Employee Assistance Program or Crisis Specialist. Our RaderCo Crisis Specialist works with clients while they are waiting to work with a counselor. She also works with teams. For example, a client had cancer, and our specialist worked with team members to talk about how they should approach it, what kind of support she may need, and what to expect.

Physical Activity Programs: Offer fitness memberships or reimbursement for classes or equipment for both in-office and remote employees.

Provide Healthy Meal Options: Always provide healthy snack options in the cafeteria, especially for meetings. Give remote employees healthy snack baskets to be delivered to their door.

Discourage Off-Hour Communication: Promote scheduling messages to be delivered during work hours or have email and chat shut off during certain hours (that's a nuclear option, but some companies do it!).

Quiet Rooms: Have a Zen Room or Quiet Space for people to sit, relax, and recharge their batteries when they need a break from people or their computers.

While our health is our responsibility, I've provided some focus areas for each role.

Levels

Action steps for Individuals:
- Take Screen-Free Lunches
- Engage in Movement Opportunities

Action steps for Managers:
- Encourage Walking Meetings or Walkie-Talkies
- Promote Healthy In-Person Meetings

Action steps for C+/Business Owners:
- Create a Culture of Wellness

INDIVIDUAL

Take Screen-Free Lunches

Growing up, many of us were no strangers to eating in front of the TV. While holidays meant gathering at the dining table, everyday meals often meant TV trays and screen time. Fast forward to adulthood, and the scenario has only escalated. With laptops, tablets, and smartphones at our fingertips, screen lunches have become a regular part of our lives. But this habit affects our meal satisfaction, productivity, and health. And for the love of pizza, don't eat on video! While I don't mind sitting across the table from you in real life, something about watching people eat on camera is awful!

People who eat lunch before a screen think they're saving time by eating while working, but they tend to make more mistakes and are slower at tasks in the afternoon because they don't get that recharge break. A survey showed that North American employees who take a screen-free lunch break report higher job satisfaction, productivity, and engagement.[81]

Problems:

Less Satisfaction: Eating while distracted means we don't fully taste or appreciate our food. It doesn't get imprinted on our brain that we've eaten, leading to more afternoon snacking and less enjoyment.

Screen Apnea: Focusing on screens can lead to shallow breathing or breath-holding, which can affect digestion and cause headaches, shoulder aches, and neck pain. Leaving your screen at lunch helps you return to a regular breathing rate.

Low Energy and Focus: Breaks are essential for recharging mentally, fostering creativity, and maintaining productivity.

---

[81] Ruchika T. Malhotra, "Take Your Lunch Break!," Harvard Business Review, January 21, 2021 (https://hbr.org/2021/01/take-your-lunch-break)

Unhappiness: There's a connection between screen usage during breaks and unhappiness.[82] Investing in true restorative time is crucial. We aren't robots. We need breaks to recharge mentally, foster creativity, and stay productive.

Solutions:

Try the 1-10-1 Approach: Start with one day. If you eat every lunch in front of a screen every day, begin with one day per week when you're screen-free, aiming to eat screen-free most days. If you can't stay away from your screen for a whole lunch, start with just the first ten minutes away from the screen. And if every meal you eat is screen-bound, begin with just one meal screen-free daily.

Block Your Calendar: Block out time daily to eat lunch and get a little movement in. If you're in the office, use this time to eat with colleagues and connect with them, or maybe you need to get out of the office and take a break.

Invite a Colleague: Getting to know a team member or another employee outside of work tasks and meetings can humanize them and help you work better together in the future.

---

[82] Drake Baer, "Hate Happiness? Then Keep Eating Lunch at Your Desk," Fast Company, October 16, 2013 (https://www.fastcompany.com/3020008/hate-happiness-then-keep-eating-lunch-at-your-desk)

Get Outside: Spending even a little time outdoors daily can lower your heart rate and blood pressure, so bonus points if you eat lunch outside![83]

Regroup: Treat lunch as sports teams treat halftime—take a few minutes to reassess your situation and re-prioritize the rest of your day based on how the morning has unfolded.

> *Kara worked remotely and felt anxious about taking time away from her desk, even though she would have lunch with colleagues when she went into the office. I convinced her to take Fridays to walk down to a favorite lunch spot for an hour. She said it made a world of difference and felt like such a treat that she looked forward to it every week.*

Screen-free lunches can be the key to a healthier lifestyle, more energy and focus in the afternoon, and a greater sense of well-being. Plus, your food just plain tastes better!

TL;DR

Ditch the screens during lunch for better health and productivity! Eating in front of screens leads to less satisfaction, overeating, and reduced productivity. Studies show that screen-free lunches improve job satisfaction, engagement, and

---

[83] "Eating Outdoors: Good for the Mind and the Soul," Cafe Dantorels, (https://cafedantorels.com/eating-outdoors-good-for-the-mind-and-the-soul/#:~:text=Less%20Stress,and%20more%20presence%20with%20others)

overall well-being. Start small by dedicating one meal or even just ten minutes screen-free and gradually increase. Embrace outdoor breaks, connect with colleagues, and use lunchtime to recharge. You'll feel more energetic and focused and enjoy your meals more.

Engage in Movement Opportunities

We all sit too much. Our bodies are not meant to be in that position for eight, ten, or 12 hours a day. The average desk worker sits for seven to *ten hours. The average kid sits for eight-plus, which should be a public health crisis!* If you work from home, your steps may be almost non-existent, especially during high heat or frigid temperatures when you don't go outside, sometimes for days! The idea is to bring more movement. Changing positions can benefit you if you prefer sitting or must sit.

Changing positions also means taking breaks or Movement Opportunities. Half of desk workers rarely or never take breaks during the work day. These workers were 1.7 times more likely to experience burnout. Colleagues who take breaks have 62% higher scores for work-life balance, are 43% better able to manage stress and anxiety and have 43% greater overall satisfaction. And...drumroll, please, *13% higher scores for productivity!*[84] If athletes need downtime to recover and "get back in the zone," why are we any different? Your brain is burning calories, too!

---

[84] "Grow Your Lunch Business with Take Back the Lunch Break," Torc USA, June 29, 2022 (https://www.torkusa.com/press-releases/tork-takes-back-lunch-break)

Risk factors of sitting too much:

- Increased risk for diabetes, heart disease, weight gain, slower metabolism, decreased blood sugar control, and obesity.

- Glute Amnesia - Our glutes, which are supposed to be the second strongest muscle in our body, start to forget how to fire or contract. And over time, they'll get so weak that they'll start pulling in accessory muscles. So we think we have a bad back or bad knees, but what we have is a *weak butt*.

- Increased neck and back pain.

- Increased stress, anxiety, and depression, especially if involving screens (that would be your computer!).

The following items can be purchased for a home office or offered as workspaces at a company office.

Options:

Sit-Stand Desk

Adjustable sit-stand desks can improve productivity, concentration, and creativity. While standing, your body's largest muscles work, increasing blood flow to the brain. This improves the way we feel and function. Standing also creates a sense of urgency and tells our brains we're working. Sitting can tell our brain we're relaxing or in leisure mode. One study found that sit-stand desks can increase productivity by 10-20%.[85] Standing keeps the back straight; with height-adjustable desks, there should be no neck craning to look up or down at a computer screen while working.

I've used a standing desk since 2007 and tend to stand all day except for meals or writing by hand. However, it's not ideal for everyone. Start using a standing desk at certain times of day for specific amounts of time or tasks. Don't start by standing all day, or you'll feel tired and sore and wonder why you ever thought this was a good idea.

- **Try to alternate frequently:** What's best for the body is not to sit or stand but to *move*. Just getting up and down burns more calories than sitting or standing alone. Try to alternate between the two positions as often as it makes sense.

- **Work on your posture:** Stand up straight when upright and keep your hips tucked under. If you're standing but leaning on one hip or hanging out with your elbows on the table, your posture may be worse than if you were sitting. Use a keyboard extender or laptop riser if you need to. Having a small stool or box that you put one foot on slightly in front of you can help by letting you shift your weight and reduce slouching while also easing pressure on your lower back and hips. Elevating one foot can also prevent any swelling and engage different muscles.

---

[85] "Benefits of Sit Stand Desks on Posture on Work Health and Well-Being," Posture Group (https://www.posturegroup.co.uk/blog/benefits-of-sit-stand-desks-on-your-posture-and-work-health-and-wellbeing)

- **Buy an anti-fatigue mat:** A cushioned mat can help ease the strain of standing, and some types come with a contour that encourages movement. When someone tells me they are buying a standing desk, my next question is, "Did you get an anti-fatigue mat?"

- **Try to stand after eating:** Do a standing period where you're slightly more active than you would be sitting to help burn a few more calories and decrease blood sugar spikes.

Pro Tip: Make sure your cables have enough slack so you don't have cable chaos every time you move your desk up and down and a cord gets pulled out of *the wall.*

"I look for movement opportunities everywhere, even just standing at my desk! If someone walks by my office and sees me marching in place, I tell them, 'I promised Marcey I'd keep this up!' When I travel for business, I organize the 6 a.m. walking club so we get in our steps before the conference starts. I incorporated a 'no excuse' policy for myself. I don't have to commit to huge amounts of exercise, but I have to do *something*. Even if I don't feel well, I can do a little bit. I usually do more than I think I will." – Deb McMurray, Associate Director, Contract Operations, Biogen

Bike Desk

I have a FitDesk bike desk. It's different from a regular bicycle because it's meant to be used while *working*. It has a smaller footprint, so it doesn't take up as much office space. You sit upright instead of hunched over, and the seat has a back. The desk part in front is slightly angled and rubberized, so your laptop doesn't slide off. I invested in the side wings to have a paper pad and a water bottle or mug beside me. I use my bike desk to watch webinars, participate in my marathon, 2.5-hour monthly mastermind calls, read long articles or papers, or during my personal time reading a book. It's not meant for getting in a workout and sweating. It's meant for *moving*. I edited a lot of this book on my Fitbike.

Treadmill desk or walking pad

Treadmill desks will take up much more space in your office, but if you have the real estate, go for it! A more reasonable option is a walking pad that can sit under your desk and easily move out of the way. Several people tell me they use a walking pad or treadmill desk while watching my webinars. Check out a walking desk if you want to walk the talk (pun intended).

Key things to note:

- If you're working on your treadmill, the proper speed is about one to two miles per hour. Like the bike desk, we aren't power walking while working, which can be distracting. We're strolling. Trust me, you are burning calories and making your muscles stronger. Here's something cool: one study found that walking increased creativity, even if the participants were staring at a blank wall while on a treadmill![86]

- Consider the noise of a treadmill. You may only be able to use it on calls that you are only listening to. If it is to be placed in a group office, it might be best in a corner or room away from other desks.

Under-desk elliptical

Don't want people to know you're moving under that desk? An under-desk elliptical or bicycle is low-profile and keeps your lower legs moving. Since it's a smaller movement, people can't tell you're doing it. You'll have to ensure you have enough room under your desk for your legs to go up and down.

Any of these items may take some coordination and time to get used to. You'll find which things work well for specific tasks and which don't. The bottom line is to test one out and get more movement in!

Movement Opportunities or Snackable Moments

Ever find yourself so swamped that you barely have time to grab a bite, let alone hit the gym? We've all been there. So let's talk about the magic of snackable moments—"snacking"—not just food-wise, but life-wise.

---

[86] Marily Oppezzo and Daniel L. Schwartz, "Learning, Memory, and Cognition: Give Your Ideas Some Legs: The Positive Effect of Walking on Creative Thinking," Journal of Experimental Psychology, 2014 (https://www.apa.org/pubs/journals/releases/xlm-a0036577.pdf)

We're all experts at food snacking, right? You're running from meeting to meeting, so you grab a banana or a protein bar. It takes a minute—maybe five—but it does the job. It sustains you. It energizes you. And guess what? We often fit these tiny munch moments into our day without a second thought.

The same goes for how we consume media. Don't have time for a three-hour epic on a Tuesday evening but still want to wind down? You opt for a 30-minute episode of your latest Netflix obsession instead. Can't listen to an entire album? A quick Spotify search for your favorite tracks will do. Quick, satisfying, and no commitment woes! *So, why not snackable moments of exercise?*

When it comes to moving our bodies, we're often stuck in an all-or-nothing mindset. No time for a 45-minute cardio session? We scrap the idea altogether. But hold on a minute— have you heard of NEAT? That's Non-Exercise Activity Thermogenesis,[87] a fancy term for all the small movements you make throughout the day. Standing, pacing, even fidgeting— it adds up, folks! In fact, NEAT is a better predictor of your longevity than that morning jog you almost skipped.

---

[87] "Non-Exercise Activity Thermogenesis," Wikipedia (https://en.wikipedia.org/wiki/Non-exercise_activity_thermogenesis)

Let's call those small exercises what they really are—Movement Opportunities[88] or Movement Snacks.[89] Imagine doing a quick set of lunges while waiting for your coffee to brew or some seated leg raises during a Zoom call. Trust me, these "exercise snacks" add up and significantly impact your well-being.

If we know a moving break makes us more productive, improves our mental health, and has all the benefits I've previously mentioned, how about...

- Incorporating more walking meetings
- Pacing during phone calls
- Keeping a set of weights or bands at your desk
- Doing a set of shoulder or neck rolls between every task

Snacking all day on food may not be great for your waistline, but snacking all day on movement can have the opposite effect...and increase your productivity to boot!

TL;DR

We all sit too much, turning into desk potatoes and risking health issues like diabetes and heart disease. The fix? Mix in some movement! Try a sit-stand desk for a boost of energy

---

[88] Marcey Rader, "Marcey Rader on Movement Opportunities for Health and Productivity," RaderCo (https://www.helloraderco. com/marcey-rader-on-movement-opportunities-for-health-and-productivity/)

[89] Marcey Rader, "Why Snackable Moments are Your New Productivity Hack," RaderCo (https://www.helloraderco.com/snackable-moments/)

and creativity, pedal away with an under-desk bike during calls, or stroll with a treadmill desk if you've got the space. Sneak in "movement snacks" like lunges during coffee breaks or stretches during Zoom calls. These small changes keep you healthy and make a big difference in your day.

MANAGER

Encourage Walking Meetings or Walkie Talkies

If you want to stand out, be more creative, and do something good for your brain and your butt, do a walking meeting! Walking meetings work best with two or three people and have been shown to increase creativity and collaboration.[90] Walking side-by-side may decrease intimidation and the real or perceived hierarchy that comes with sitting across from someone at a desk.

Inviting someone to walk can burn a few calories, give your eyes a break from the screen, and lower stress levels.

Many leaders have utilized this method.[91]

---

[90] Marily Oppezzo and Daniel L. Schwartz, "Learning, Memory, and Cognition: Give Your Ideas Some Legs: The Positive Effect of Walking on Creative Thinking," Journal of Experimental Psychology, 2014 (https://www.apa.org/pubs/journals/releases/xlm-a0036577.pdf)

[91] Jessica Gross, "Walking Meetings? 5 Surprising Thinkers Who Swore by Them," TED Blog, April 29, 2013 (https://blog.ted.com/walking-meetings-5-surprising-thinkers-who-swore-by-them/#:~:text=Steve%20Jobs%20made%20a%20habit,to%20have%20a%20serious%20conversation.%E2%80%9D)

Steve Jobs: Taking a long walk was his preferred method for serious conversation, especially if it was the first time he was meeting you.

Sigmund Freud: He conducted consultations and met with patients while walking.

Aristotle: He instructed students while walking.

My friend Melina Palmer, behavioral economist a*nd host of The Brainy Business Podcast,* does walking meetings with her husband and Chief Operating Officer, sometimes clocking 20-30 miles in a week!

Todd Rader, my brother and President of B&M Steel, has a large basement where he walks laps while he talks. He has gotten 2,500-5,000 steps while doing business!

When I meet with our Client Concierge Lisa, each quarter for our two-day reflection and planning retreats, we clock in nine to 15 miles, alternating walking with computer time.

Guidelines for walking meetings:

- **Make sure it's in an area you know** – This is not the time for exploring or getting lost.

- **Consider the time of day and weather** – July at 1:00 p.m. in North Carolina or any time in February in Minnesota may not be ideal outside walking times.

- **Ask the person ahead of time if they are okay with doing a moving meeting** – Don't surprise them with one when they are wearing a suit or three-inch heels.

- **Keep it short and stroll** – This is not the time to demonstrate your physical prowess or how fast you can walk a mile. Check the pace and be mindful of your meeting partner's breathing to ensure they aren't dying inside while you are skipping along. When I started doing these over a decade ago, I often walked too fast for people and learned later that I had given them a workout while I was just "taking a walk." Now, I always check in and allow them to set the pace, knowing that I walk faster than most people (picture the Road Runner with fidget-spinning legs here, "meep meep!").

- **Remote? You can still do walkie-talkies by phone** – Sometimes, taking a meeting this way can help you pay *more* attention since you don't have the distraction of the computer in front of you. If you live in a loud area, be mindful of the noise and decide if it's best for calls where you mostly listen. When I schedule virtual coffees with people, I always give them an option of phone or video and will often do these meetings while walking if they choose the phone. About half the time, they put on their shoes and walk, too.

But what about note-taking?

If you're worried that you may want to take notes during a meeting, bring along a small pad of paper and jot down action items or things you want to follow up on. I sometimes stop momentarily, jot a note or two, or text myself, and then pick back up, but I often find that this kind of talking meeting doesn't require notes.

Ideal walking meetings are with friends at work, one-to-ones with direct reports, meetings with referral partners, or sales calls, especially if you know the person is interested in their health. One credit card processing company owner who had attended one of my workshops closed a multi-million-dollar deal during an in-person walking meeting. To be memorable, why not do something besides coffee, lunch, or drinks?

My favorite walkie-talkie story happened at a biotech company in Boston. I was coaching a director considering firing a team member who had made a million-dollar mistake. The director felt sick about it. During our coaching session that day, I encouraged her to have the conversation as a walking meeting to get them out of the office environment and away from curious eyes. When her direct report was in nature walking, it reduced her nervousness and anxiety. It relieved the adrenaline, and she felt less "on the spot" because she didn't have to look at her boss. She was more open and honest. Also, her boss is a very tall woman. The intimidation factor can be felt more with a boss (or anyone) taller than you. Afterward, the direct report commented that she was thankful that the meeting was outside while walking. Happy ending? You bet! The employee remained with the company.

Another one of my favorite examples comes from someone who participated in one of my Manage Well Remotely presentations. Matt Findley, Home & Land Lending Manager for Horizon Farm Credit, sent me this email after attending a RaderCo training:

"In your presentation, you stressed the importance of being disconnected from technology when conversing, thus allowing yourself not to be distracted. Once your training was completed, you and I discussed how we thought this would work with individual check-ins. Soon after, our management group had the opportunity to sit down with our teams and discuss three- to five-year plans for where they would like to go and how we, as leadership, can help them accomplish this goal.

I allowed each team member to have the meeting as a walking meeting, face-to-face or virtual.

I asked the team members who chose walking meetings to come prepared to walk and not wear work attire. I also allowed them to select the location to meet.

We would start walking, and I would talk with them for the first five minutes. During these five minutes,

I took this as an opportunity to help explain the why. Why was this important to them, me, and Farm Credit? I also talked with them about our meeting and your shared impact on walking and disconnecting. Finally, I spoke with them about the importance of the symbolism of walking side by side. My definition was, I am not standing in front of you leading you to where you think you need to go, I am not walking behind you to push you to where I think you need to be, I am walking next to you on this journey, and I'm here to support you along the way.

After those first five minutes, I had the opportunity to sit back and listen by asking one simple question: What's on your mind?

By asking this question, I was blessed with information on everything from family life to the struggles they were facing personally and professionally and the good, bad, and sometimes ugly of everyday life that affects us all.

Some of these conversations went on for miles, yes, miles. Most averaged two miles, and the furthest we walked was four miles in 98-degree heat (I think he wanted to find out if I was for real). Yes, I was for real. Once our discussion was completed, we found a bench (still not at the office) and did a read-back. We sat down, and I started writing notes. Then, once I completed a thought, I would follow up with them by saying, 'This is what I heard you say. Was this your intent in this conversation?' This allowed them to have final input and allowed me not to place my biases on the conversation.

Every one of my teammates who selected the walking meeting has told me this is how they want to have check-ins from here on out. I have had multiple walking meetings since this check-in and have really bonded with my team. One employee said the meeting filled his 'cup of trust' with me. I told him that was inspiring to hear because now he knows that my requests of him don't come from a place of malice or distrust but from a place of need."

Want to track your steps and raise money at the same time? The Charity Miles app (www.charitymiles.org) integrates with Outlook, allowing you to schedule a one-to-one walking meeting. While you're using it, you're also raising money for charity!

TL;DR

Walking meetings are a great way to boost creativity, collaboration, and productivity while getting some physical activity. Walking side-by-side reduces intimidation and hierarchy, making conversations more open. Many leaders, like Steve Jobs and Sigmund Freud, preferred walking meetings. They can burn calories, lower stress, and give your eyes a break from screens. Plan the route, consider the weather, and check with participants beforehand for optimal results. Walking meetings are ideal for one-to-ones, brainstorming, and virtual meetings.

Promote Healthy In-Person Meetings

Meetings don't have to be a drag—they can be healthy, energizing, and even fun! As managers and leaders, we can transform those stuffy, energy-draining, sedentary sessions filled with too much coffee and sugar into dynamic, wellness-boosting events. This section explores how we can make in-person meetings, especially those half-day or full-day offsites or all-company meetings, healthier with well-timed breaks and smart food choices.

> *"Marcey asked great questions to assess our needs, pre-surveyed the participants for their insights, and developed a customized program matching our expectations. Her Health and Personal Productivity series was appropriate and applicable to many different levels in our firm. As a professional, Marcey exudes confidence and energy in her delivery and instruction while bringing fresh and exciting perspectives to motivate our associates." – Karen McManus, Vice President, Employee Success*

Problems:

Too long: Long, uninterrupted work sessions often produce less-than-stellar results. When people are tired or have decision fatigue, they may resort to status quo or fear-based decisions. They may also think about all their work piling up, be anxious to finish and return to *work, and disrespectfully agree (agreeing when they really don't want to)* to get back to their desks.[92]

---

[92] Justin Jones-Fosu, I Respectfully Disagree: How to Have Difficult Conversations in a Divided World, April 16, 2024, Berrett-Koehler Publishers (https://www.amazon.com/Respectfully-Disagree-Difficult-Conversations-Divided/dp/152300651X)

Sitting: People get tired and uncomfortable from sitting, especially since they often aren't in their ergonomic desk chairs. Since I'm 5'2", I find conference tables too high, so if I have my chair up high enough, my feet are dangling. If I lower it enough that my feet touch the ground, then I look like a child.

Junk Food Frenzy: All those donuts, bagels, cookies, and coffee are going to spike everyone's blood sugar and then bottom it out, crashing and sucking the energy from the room.

Over-caffeinated: Coffee and soda flow all day, temporarily increasing energy but then dropping *you* back below normal levels. It's a vicious cycle that leads to low energy.

Mental Overload: Putting too many topics on the agenda is a common pitfall and can make people feel rushed to get to them all. When all topics aren't covered, it feels like a failed meeting.

Stale Spaces: A dark, windowless room doesn't inspire creativity. If you meet in the office, people can also get distracted by non-meeting-attending colleagues or other work matters.

Solutions:

Break it up! Schedule a quick break every hour or so. Get a timing system you can put on the table, like the Time Timer (timetimer.com). Set it for 50 minutes and take a ten-minute break each hour. The countdown clock may also create urgency and remind people to stick to the topic agenda. During the break, encourage everyone to stretch or move. Ask your team to avoid looking at their phones or emails between meeting sessions, especially if you don't often get everyone together in one room. As a result, your team will return sharper and more focused.

Walkie-Talkies or Standing Sprints: If brainstorming or problem-solving sessions are scheduled, break your team into groups and assign two or three people to walk and talk together. We know by now that walking makes us more creative. You can also make some parts of the meeting standing. Invite everyone who can to stand up for one section or agenda item. One client, Emaar Properties, has treadmill desks facing each other in some of their meeting spaces and high tables with no chairs to encourage movement and standing while meeting. One space I saw had three meeting rooms with only a whiteboard, not even a table, which meant that everyone had to stand. This also prevented people from using their computers during the meeting, so they had to focus. Standing meetings also tend to be shorter.

> "I've always loved brainstorming with others to solve challenges and come up with new business ideas. Marcey's plan to have a walking meeting—instead of my traditional sit-around-a-table session—was a refreshing and energizing change of pace. I was able to work through a challenge that had been plaguing me for two years, and I am now implementing a solution to serve a new market." – Nika Stewart, CEO of Streambank Media

Provide healthy food options: Swap out the refined, sugary carbs for higher protein, higher fiber foods. Think fruits, hard-boiled eggs, yogurt, cottage cheese, and nuts for breakfast and vegetables and protein for lunch. Whatever you do, don't put cookies or donuts in the middle of the table. Food is an emotional decision for some people. They will spend the whole meeting only thinking about that cookie and whether they should eat it. Then, there will be a mental fight about whether they should eat a second one, the equivalent of a Golden Gloves boxing match. Your meeting will be the last thing on their minds. Ideally, have the food outside the room. And when you say you will break for lunch, stay on time. They no longer care about the meeting once they know the food is there or it's time for lunch, according to your agenda.

Consider Food Sensitivities and Restrictions: If you can eat anything you want, congratulations! Not everyone can. Please be mindful and poll your attendees on any food restrictions. Everyone should be accommodated with something that resembles a meal. That means if you have someone gluten-free or a vegetarian, they get more than iceberg lettuce with a few carrot shavings. Spend a few extra bucks if you need to. It's not worth the price of the resentment from being excluded.

Hydration Station: Keep the H2O flowing. Offer water, maybe with a twist of lemon or cucumber, herbal teas, or fun drinks like kombucha. Provide a non-alcoholic bar or mocktail hour mid-afternoon or after you're done. Hydrated brains think better!

Mix Up the Agenda: Change your topics so you don't hit all the challenging ones back-to-back. Alternate between intense discussions and lighter topics. Toss in a quick breathing exercise (look one up on YouTube or use an app) or group stretching to reset after each topic.

Engaging Space: Opt for meeting rooms with natural light and good airflow. Book a room at a coworking space or hotel, but ask for a room with windows. Better yet, take it outside if you can. If the weather is nice, go outside to picnic tables or a pavilion. We did a half-day Vistage meeting outside at a pavilion once, and it was such a great change of pace! Fresh air and a change of scenery work wonders.

TL;DR

In-person, half-day, or all-day meetings don't have to be a drain. Break up long sessions with hourly breaks, add standing or walking discussions, and provide healthy snacks like fruits and nuts instead of sugary treats. Offer water and herbal teas to avoid caffeine crashes, mix up the agenda with intense and lighter topics, use meeting rooms with natural light, or even take it outside. These changes boost productivity and team well-being.

C+/BUSINESS OWNER

Create a Culture of Wellness

Creating a healthy workplace isn't just about gym memberships and salad bars. It's about cultivating an environment where employees thrive physically, mentally, and emotionally. The right mix of innovative strategies can transform a company culture, boost productivity, and keep your team engaged and happy. The words self-care are all over social media, and people know they need to take better care of themselves, but it's not just the individual's responsibility. It's the company's, too. Wellness is not just about adding "cool" perks like unlimited cold brew or Zen rooms. It's about rethinking the work culture that necessitates all this self-care in the first place.

Here at RaderCo, we get an insider's look at all sorts of wellness amenities—everything from Employee Assistance Programs (EAPs) and virtual yoga classes to in-house massage therapists. Kudos to the companies for making these offerings available, but let's not forget one thing: all the perks in the world won't matter if employees don't have the time or mental bandwidth to use them.

Would you even need a two-minute meditation from the insurance-provided app if you weren't trying to get work done sandwiched between back-to-back video meetings? Would you require an in-house therapist if your company culture didn't keep you on edge 24/7?

Failures we've seen

The companies mentioned are anonymous, but the struggles are real.

1. **Company A:** An insurance provider slashed healthcare benefits but promoted a meditation app now included in their plan. Our coaching client spent hours calling offices *to find a covered psychiatrist who was actually taking patients* for her 13-year-old son, who was being bullied. Stressing over healthcare needs? That meditation app is suddenly less appealing.

2. **Company B:** A global biotech company offers acupuncture and chiropractic benefits but won't

cough up a dime for an ergonomic desk. One expectant mom, who was supposed to be on a hybrid work schedule, chose to work from home 100% of the time to use her sit-stand desk to avoid discomfort—all because of a missing $150 standing desk in her corporate office. She also had to endure the shaming from her team because she "got" to work entirely from home during the last five months of her pregnancy. She even had a doctor's note!

Success Stories

Alright, enough of the downer stuff. Let's talk wins. A hospital fundraising team at the University of North Carolina, Chapel Hill, that we worked with for a year, opted to spend their "office party" budget on productivity workshops and coaching over the typical celebratory gatherings and group lunches. The result? A more cohesive, efficient, and stress-free work environment. You can learn more by reading the UNC Health Foundation case study at helloraderco.com/case-study/team-coaching-success-story.

Another client, Cook Wealth, reduced internal meetings and actually encouraged their team to—wait for it—enjoy nature walks together! And leaders led them! Read the case study summary at helloraderco.com/cook-wealth-case-study.

Lastly, our client, Blueprint Medicines, offers RaderCo productivity coaching packages that are integral to their enablement strategy. This ensures that every employee can signal their interest and make a case for personalized coaching regardless of their level. This benefit is not just for executives and leaders. It's for everyone because if the people supporting the leaders aren't effective, happy, and healthy, it hurts the whole organization and brings bottlenecks of a different type. Meaningful behavior change and other benefits of coaching also often create additional opportunities to drive impactful growth and development.

We've implemented Design Days (https://www.helloraderco.com/design-days/) there too, where most of the company is meeting-, email-, and instant-message-free three times per year to allow everyone to engage in deep, focused work.

Blueprint Medicines also offers acute crisis counseling with our RaderCo Crisis Specialist, Becky Sansbury, for team members who have experienced life crises of various forms. This is important because, while long-term therapy may be needed, the energy to find a therapist or counselor in your plan (if it's even covered), get on a waitlist, or schedule an appointment, and then wait for that appointment is too much to bear and not helpful in a moment of crisis. Offering this option within 24-72 hours, with the expectation of one session or a few until the person can find long-term help, is invaluable to the employee and not a burden to coordinate. Read the case study at helloraderco.com/blueprint-medicines-case-study.

> "There are practical, doable ways for ordinary people to support a colleague during a crisis. This does not require counseling training. It requires openness to training, team communication, and consistent action. I was initially hired by an organization to provide one-on-one crisis coaching to an employee struggling with his child's severe illness. The situation became so intense, the employee had to take a medical leave of absence. With the employee's permission, I remained

in touch with his manager and encouraged her to send short, consistent messages of encouragement. She was eager to support her team member, but didn't know what to say. I provided a list of phrases that have helped others, which gave her the confidence to get started. When the situation had resolved, the employee was anxious about what his team might ask or say to him when he returned to work. The company approved my facilitating a discussion between his manager and the employee about what might help to ease the awkwardness for everyone. We developed a list of topics that were 'okay' and those to be avoided in office conversations, setting clear, personal boundaries regarding the employee's situation. Then I drafted an email with this list. The employee sent it to his colleagues the day before his return to work. These conversations and actions assisted the affected employee, the manager, and the other team members during and after the crisis."
– Becky Sansbury, RaderCo Executive Crisis Specialist

Finally, while many companies offer a cookie-cutter approach to wellness benefits, I like that Blueprint Medicines provides an allowance via a Lifestyle Spending Account that people can use for various categories, such as Wellness Apps, Meals and Nutrition, Home Cleaning, and Repair Services, and even Pet Care! They even have a free mobile information service to promote maternal and child health.

A Call to Leaders

If you're in a leadership role, ask yourself: "What workplace pressures are making my team members desperately need that #SelfCare?" Self-care shouldn't be a burden on the individual or the team. Let's make it something more genuine, more integrated, and ultimately more **effective**.

Problems:

Sedentary Lifestyles: Stuck at desks all day, employees risk turning into office zombies, with health issues like obesity and heart disease creeping in, affecting their overall well-being and costs in lost productivity and increased health care expenses.[93]

Poor Food Choices: Vending machines, fast food for group meals, sodas, bagels, and donuts can make anyone crash hard from the sugar and refined, processed food. Also, food can be an emotional decision and distraction for people trying to make healthy choices.

---

[93] Edward R. Laskowski, MD, "What Are the Risks of Sitting Too Much," The Mayo Clinic (https://www.mayoclinic.org/healthy-lifestyle/adult-health/expert-answers/sitting/faq-20058005#:~:text=Too%20much%20sitting%20overall%20and,from%20cardiovascular%20disease%20and%20cancer)

True Story

I was working out of a corporate office with an audit team and received a mass email reminding us that we would celebrate a team member's birthday by meeting in the breakroom for cake. I didn't know him well but wanted to show my team spirit. Here's the *scenario...*

Birthday Guy walks into the meeting room. There are about ten people there, and we sing 'Happy Birthday.' A team member cuts the cake and starts to divvy it up. Most partake, and a few decline. The guy whose birthday we were celebrating asked for a tiny piece. He takes one small bite and throws it away, hoping no one saw him. I asked him if he liked cake. He quietly said he was on a 'no sugar' diet and didn't want it. I could tell he felt guilty for even saying that. The worst part of this whole party was that several people knew he was watching his sugar intake! Even the woman who bought the cake! That was the rudest and most selfish thing I can imagine on a birthday. She shrugged when I mentioned it and said everyone else would eat it.

Seriously? We were not celebrating this guy at all. The office just used his birthday as an excuse to buy cake! This guy wanted an

> acknowledgment or a song, something he liked to eat, or maybe nothing at all.
>
> I have almost always worked remotely, and being part of that birthday scene made me feel glad on so many levels. No one should feel guilty on their birthday or any other day of the year for not eating *something*, especially when the person giving it to you knows you don't like it. If you are someone who pressures people to eat the dessert or drink the wine in order to make yourself feel better, take an emotional inventory. If you want those things, have them and enjoy! The whole table doesn't have to join you.

Chronic Stress Levels: Chronic stress can turn even the best employees into frazzled bundles of nerves. Consider what's happening upstream in your processes, causing them to need a mid-week yoga class. At best, this is a band-aid fix. Is your team stressed because of their workload? Are they experiencing the anticipatory stress of getting an email after hours? Is it your always-on culture? Implementing efficiencies upstream will create downstream effects, where they won't need as many trendy office wellness perks.

An Always-On Culture: At RaderCo, we don't really use the term work-life balance. What most people need is tech-life balance. If employees feel like they must always be on, it creates microstressors during off-hours, making them feel that they are constantly falling behind or must be available. This trickles down to their families, too, creating anticipatory stress that mom or dad may get a text or email that will take them away or distract them. Also, overloaded meeting schedules mean people are doing their "real work" at night, which interrupts their sleep and causes isolation from family members. Digital overload from constant screen time = fried brains and unhealthy bodies.

Dreary Work Environment: An office with lousy lighting and uncomfortable furniture can drain energy and productivity faster than a caffeine crash. Although open-concept office environments are trendy and less costly, they are a disaster for deep, focused work. Employees are more distracted by other people talking, feel like they don't have any privacy, and are often *less likely* to engage with co-workers! They will opt to go somewhere private to have a conversation or get focused work done.

Solutions:

Moving Offices: I'm not talking about relocating across town, but rather having workstations where people can move around. Sit-stand desks, high-top tables, bike desks, treadmill desks, or walking pads are options around the company for people to work at for an hour or two throughout the day. These options can give people new scenery, boost energy, and increase creativity.

Provide Healthy Food Options: Stock the kitchen with healthy snacks. Be inclusive by offering food for those with restrictions (gluten-free, vegetarian or vegan, nut allergies, etc.). Be mindful of all-company lunches and whether they will cause low energy in the afternoon.

Be Flexible: Offer flexible work schedules outside of core hours. Not everyone works best between 8 a.m. and 5 p.m.

Maybe have core hours of 9 a.m. to 3 p.m. or 10 a.m. to 2 p.m., and the rest of their work time can be whenever that person feels at their best. I'm an early-morning person, and my husband is a night owl. Accommodating our schedules means you'll get more out of us, and we'll be happier, too.

Mandatory Time Off: Encourage real vacations where employees actually unplug and recharge. See Chapter 6 for more about how to make taking vacation and time off a reality. Discourage people from sending emails outside of traditional office hours or make it mandatory that no one sends emails outside of traditional office hours (this only works for some companies that don't work across time zones).

Work Environment: Invest in ergonomic furniture, better lighting, plants or a living plant wall, and quiet spaces. If you're in an open-concept office, create cubbies and Zoom booths (telephone booths) for people to have a calm workspace. Have areas outside with picnic tables or covered pavilions, too.

> *"I can only imagine—if your entire organization could bring in RaderCo, you would be unstoppable."*
> *– Matt Bailey*

TL;DR

Creating a healthy workplace isn't just about gym memberships and salad bars. It's about cultivating an environment where employees thrive physically, mentally, and emotionally. Instead of piling on "cool" perks like cold brew or Zen rooms (although those are awesome!), rethink the work culture that necessitates self-care in the first place. Focus on core issues like workload, tech-life balance, and supportive environments. The right strategies can transform your culture.

References

Drake Baer, "Hate Happiness? Then Keep Eating Lunch at Your Desk," Fast Company, October 16, 2013 (https://www.fastcompany.com/3020008/hate-happiness-then-keep-eating-lunch-at-your-desk)

Kara Dennison, "Why companies should prioritize employee health and happiness in 2024," Forbes, October 24, 2023 (https://www.forbes.com/sites/karadennison/2023/10/24/why-companies-should-prioritize-employee-health-and-happiness-in-2024/)

Justin Jones-Fosu, I Respectfully Disagree: How to Have Difficult Conversations in a Divided World, April 16, 2024, Berrett-Koehler Publishers (https://www.amazon.com/Respectfully-Disagree-Difficult-Conversations-Divided/dp/152300651X)

Edward R. Laskowski, MD, "What Are the Risks of Sitting Too Much," The Mayo Clinic (https://www.mayoclinic.org/healthy-lifestyle/adult-health/expert-answers/sitting/faq-20058005#:~:text=Too%20much%20sitting%20overall%20and,from%20cardiovascular%20disease%20and%20cancer)

Ruchika T. Malhotra, "Take Your Lunch Break!," Harvard Business Review, January 21, 2021 (https://hbr.org/2021/01/take-your-lunch-break)

Marily Oppezzo and Daniel L. Schwartz, "Learning, Memory, and Cognition: Give Your Ideas Some Legs: The Positive Effect of Walking on Creative Thinking," Journal of Experimental Psychology, 2014 (https://www.apa.org/pubs/journals/releases/xlm-a0036577.pdf)

Marcey Rader, "Marcey Rader on Movement Opportunities for Health and Productivity," RaderCo https://www.helloraderco.com/marcey-rader-on-movement-opportunities-for-health-and-productivity/

Marcey Rader, "Why Snackable Moments are Your New Productivity Hack," RaderCo https://www.helloraderco.com/snackable-moments/

"Benefits of Sit Stand Desks on Posture on Work Health and Well-Being," Posture Group (https://www.posturegroup.co.uk/blog/benefits-of-sit-stand-desks-on-your-posture-and-work-health-and-wellbeing)

"Eating Outdoors: Good for the Mind and the Soul," Cafe Dantorels, (https://cafedantorels.com/eating-outdoors-good-for-the-mind-and-the-soul/#:~:text=Less%20Stress,and%20more%20presence%20with%20others)

"Grow Your Lunch Business with Take Back the Lunch Break," Torc USA, June 29, 2022 (https://www.torkusa.com/press-releases/tork-takes-back-lunch-break)

"Non-Exercise Activity Thermogenesis," Wikipedia (https://en.wikipedia.org/wiki/Non-exercise_activity_thermogenesis)

CHAPTER 8

PUTTING IT ALL TOGETHER

You've now read many strategies to transform how you work, lead, and live, and have a lot to choose from on the buffet. Let's put it all together with a clear, actionable plan.

Step 1: Top Three Takeaways

First, pick the three most impactful ideas to work on to reclaim your workday. Your brain loves three—so do I! Write them down, and align them with your goals.

Examples:

- Focus: Deep work blocks allow people to work in their zones of genius
- Communication: Having a communications matrix will cut down on time spent hunting for information
- Innovation: Design Days will encourage creative thinking across the organization

Step 2: Personal Action Plan

1. **Prioritize:** Start with what moves the needle most.
2. **Set Goals:** Make them clear and measurable. *Example: Cut time spent in meetings by 20% in 30 days.*
3. **Schedule:** Block time in your calendar. Consistency is key.
4. **Engage:** Bring your team into the plan. Collaborate and adapt together.

Step 3: Monitor and Adjust

1. **Weekly Review:** Spend 10-15 minutes assessing what's working.
2. **Monthly Check-In:** Evaluate your progress. Are you more focused and efficient?
3. **Team Feedback:** Ensure changes are benefiting everyone. P.S. The Powered Path Playbook® is your perfect tracking tool!

Step 4: Celebrate Wins

Acknowledge small victories—better workflows, reduced stress, energized teams. These are critical milestones.

Step 5: Continuous Improvement

Health-Powered Productivity™ is ongoing. Keep revisiting these principles to stay agile and adaptable.

Final Thought: This chapter is your guidepost. Use it to create a sustainable system that supports your goals and keeps you and your team productive and healthy.

TL;DR:

Summarize your top takeaways, create a personalized action plan, and implement strategies that align with your goals. Regularly review progress, engage your team, celebrate small (and big!) wins, and commit to continuous improvement for sustained productivity and well-being.

Next Steps

You've taken the first step toward reclaiming your workday by reading this book. High fives and fist bumps! Now, let's take it further.

Partner with RaderCo

Ready to implement these strategies across your team or organization? RaderCo is here to help you turn these ideas into action.

What We Offer

Team Training: Customized programs that tackle your team's specific productivity challenges. Whether it's mastering email management, running effective meetings, or building a culture of focus, we've got you covered.

Consulting: We work with leadership teams to design and implement systems that drive efficiency and well-being. From meeting resets to Design Days and communications matrices, we'll help you create lasting change.

Coaching: Our one-to-one coaching provides tailored support to help you or your team members achieve peak performance. Whether you're a busy executive, a manager juggling multiple roles, or an individual contributor needing guidance, we're here to elevate your productivity game.

Powered Path Program™: Your reflection, prioritization, and planning solution. The course is designed to be completed on a weekend, a day, or even an afternoon—at your pace. The program includes a digital Powered Path Playbook® to track your progress.

Say Hello to RaderCo

Visit helloraderco.com to learn more about how we can support you, your team, or your entire organization.

Ready to take your next step? Whether through team training, consulting, coaching, or the Powered Path Program™, we're here to support your journey to Health-Powered Productivity™.

Get Started:

- Visit helloraderco.com to explore our offerings.
- Learn more about Marcey Rader at marceyrader. com.

Discussion Questions

Whether you're reading *Reclaim Your Workday* with a team, a book club, or just a group of productivity-minded peers, these discussion questions are designed to spark meaningful conversations and actionable insights. Use them to reflect on your work habits, explore new strategies, and share ideas on making sustainable changes to help you reclaim your workday and boost productivity.

For those wanting even more hands-on guidance within their company, consider investing in *Reclaim Your Workday Live* with Marcey Rader. Jumpstart productivity as you navigate each chapter together with short, impactful strategies focused on sustainable, actionable results in real time. It's a collaborative, experimental approach to testing and applying the productivity techniques *directly to your team or company.* Reach out at reclaim@helloraderco.com for more details.

Remember, the goal isn't just to discuss—it's to inspire action. Dive in, reflect, and get ready to implement real change!

Focus and Distractions: What strategies from the book have you found most effective for maintaining focus in a world full of distractions? How can you apply these in both your personal and professional life?

Email and Chat Messaging: How will you adjust your approach after reading the chapter on managing email and chat? What changes can you implement in your team's communication processes?

Meetings: How have ineffective meetings impacted your productivity? Which of the suggested meeting strategies do you plan to implement in your organization, and why?

Task and Project Management: What task management technique from the book resonated most with you? How do you see it improving your workday efficiency?

Healthy Habits: The book highlights the importance of incorporating healthy habits into daily routines (Health-Powered Productivity™). What's one habit you are committed to changing or adding to improve your productivity and well-being?

Design Days: Have you tried incorporating "Design Days" or similar focused time into your schedule? How can you introduce this concept to your team or company to promote deeper work and innovation?

Leadership and Remote Work: For those in leadership positions, what steps can you take to create a more sustainable, trusting, and supportive culture, especially in a remote or hybrid work environment?

Reflection and Takeaways: What is your biggest takeaway from *Reclaim Your Workday,* and how do you plan to implement it immediately?

ACKNOWLEDGMENTS

Disclaimer: My gratitude could be another book, and I'm paranoid I would leave someone out, so I'm only acknowledging people who directly contributed in some way.

To Justin Jones-Fosu, who casually dropped the "You need to write a book for teams" bomb at the Certified Speaking Professionals® Summit in 2023. I cursed, grumbled, kicked, screamed... and then admitted you were right. You're one of the most extreme humans I know—in the best way possible. Your energy, determination, dance moves, and smile light up every room. Lucky to call you a friend? Beyond.

To Emily Crookston, my developmental editor, who can whisk a book to Nashville and microwave a manuscript in record time.

To Brett Hilker, my book coach, for being a sounding board and voice of reason. I had no idea what I'd signed up for, but I can't imagine this book without your guidance.

To Caroline and Roland Siverson, whose garden cottage became my TEDx rehearsal stage and creative sanctuary to write this book. It's the perfect spot for inspiration, just a hop, skip, and jump from home.

To Sara Shelp, one of my first clients, a brave beta reader, and someone who never interrupts my Marcey Morning Magic Time. You inspire me in ways you don't even realize. May all the coffee, wild ponies, and sound sleep you desire be yours.

To Christina Rowe for beta reading, helping me navigate my strengths and talk through difficult conversations, letting me crash at your place when you barely knew me, and that unforgettable trip to the carnivore sanctuary.

To my RaderCo Team Specialists quoted in the book: Wendy Gates Corbett, Judith Guertin, Elisabeth Galperin, Becky Sansbury, Rijul Arora, Helen Moses, Amanda Chay, Dawn Bjork, Dawn Sander, Lisa Wood, and Jennifer McCluskey, who continue to teach me and deliver heartfelt value to our clients. Your insights made the book even better.

To my clients quoted in the book, especially Blueprint Medicines and Cook Wealth—thank you for trusting me. You've made this journey exciting.

To the baristas who fueled these pages with iced concoctions— this book is basically half caffeine.

To Grammarly, the unsung hero, silently saving me from grammar catastrophes.

AUTHOR BIO

Marcey Rader is a leading expert in Health-Powered Productivity™ and a sought-after keynote speaker, trainer, coach, and author. Once caught in the relentless chase for more—more promotions, certifications, and endurance races—Marcey's perspective on success radically shifted after two preventable medical diagnoses.

As the founder of RaderCo, she has helped Fortune 500 companies, startups, and global organizations transform productivity and well-being, reaching over 100,000 people across five continents. A multi-award-winning speaker, one of only 850 Certified Speaking Professionals® in the world, a Virtual Master Presenter®, and a TEDx speaker, Marcey's expertise is widely recognized.

She has authored four books, created The Powered Path Program™ for reflection, prioritization, and planning, and been featured in Money, Inc., Shape, and Prevention. Marcey's mission is to help individuals and companies focus on what truly matters—building sustainable habits that clear the way for success in work and life—and reclaim their workdays.

She lives in Raleigh, North Carolina, where you can find her doing walking meetings, drinking iced coffee, and watching live music.

Connect with Marcey at marceyrader.com, helloraderco.com, or on LinkedIn.

BONUS RESOURCES!

Want to supercharge your book experience and unlock even more value? Readers who snag our complimentary bonus guide implement and reach their goals faster!

Sign up at reclaimyourworkday.com

Get instant access to our Reclaim Your Workday Go-To Guide with:

- Links to podcast training episodes under 20 minutes to listen to alone or to use as discussion prompts for your team
- The link to a sample Communications Matrix
- Links to bonus videos with actionable tips
- Information on how RaderCo can support you, your team, or your company

Download now and start reclaiming your workday!

Don't miss out! Get your free copy at reclaimyourworkday.com

WANT MORE?

Discover the key to a balanced, fulfilling life with my book

Work Well. Play More! Productive, Clutter-Free, Healthy-Living: One Step at a Time.

Named one of the top three books of 2023 by The Brainy Business!

This essential guide will revolutionize your approach to productivity, decluttering, and health without overwhelming you with rigid rules. Whether you're looking to boost your focus, streamline your email management, or create healthier habits, this book provides practical, adaptable steps for every aspect of your life.

Learn how to:

- Simplify your life by mastering productivity, reducing clutter, and embracing healthy living with incremental changes.
- Manage distractions, optimize meeting productivity, and set effective boundaries.
- Tackle digital, physical, and mental clutter.
- Cultivate healthy eating, regular exercise, mindful sleep, and stress management for overall well-being.

With tips categorized by difficulty (Novice, Pro, Master), you can customize your journey, selecting strategies that resonate with you. Praised by experts for its practical, real-life solutions to engage in over a year, this book is your gateway to a more organized, productive, and healthier life. Plus, access a wealth of bonus materials and resources online to support your transformation. Join countless others who have found a path to success with these transformative insights.

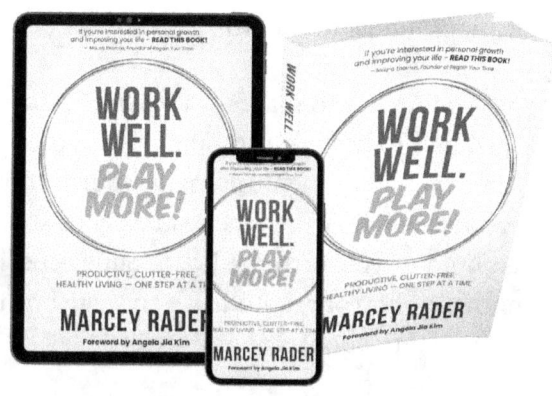

SOS REVIEW NEEDED!

First things first, you're awesome for finishing my book—thank you! Now, I've got a little favor to ask (and it's not just because I need an ego boost). Your honest review on Amazon and/or Goodreads would mean the world. It's like giving my book a little magic boost in the world of words.

If you've got two minutes to spare (or the time it takes to brush your teeth), I'd love to hear your thoughts. Whether you loved it, liked it, or even had a "meh" moment, your feedback helps other readers decide if it's worth the read. Special shout-out for including a photo of you with the book. Super-special shout-out with another dollop of gratitude if you write one thing you changed because of the book in your review!

reclaimyourworkday.com/amazon
reclaimyourworkday.com/goodreads

Thanks a million!
Marcey

www.ingramcontent.com/pod-product-compliance
Lightning Source LLC
Chambersburg PA
CBHW071719120626
46550CB00001B/299